MORE THAN

100

Brain-Friendly

TOOLS AND STRATEGIES FOR

Literacy
Instruction

This book is dedicated to my fabulous family!
To my dear husband, Robert, for always encouraging
and supporting me through the chapters of my life
To my sensational sons, Hart and Devon, for giving
me a whole new outlook on teaching and learning

MORE THAN 100

Brain-Friendly

TOOLS AND STRATEGIES FOR

Literacy
Instruction

Kathy Perez

CORWIN PRESS
A SAGE Company
Thousand Oaks, CA 91320

For information:

Corwin Press
A SAGE Company
2455 Teller Road
Thousand Oaks, California 91320
www.corwinpress.com

SAGE Ltd.
1 Oliver's Yard
55 City Road
London EC1Y 1SP
United Kingdom

SAGE India Pvt. Ltd.
B 1/I 1 Mohan Cooperative
    Industrial Area
Mathura Road, New Delhi 110 044
India

SAGE Asia-Pacific Pte. Ltd.
33 Pekin Street #02-01
Far East Square
Singapore 048763

Printed in the United States of America.

Library of Congress Cataloging-in-Publication Data

Perez, Katherine.
More than 100 brain-friendly tools and strategies for literacy instruction/Katherine Perez.
    p. cm.
Includes bibliographical references and index.
ISBN 978-1-4129-2692-8 (cloth)
ISBN 978-1-4129-2693-5 (pbk.)
    1. Reading—Aids and devices. I. Title. II. Title: More than one hundred brain-friendly tools and strategies for literacy instruction.

LB1573.39.P52 2008
372.41—dc22   2008001242

This book is printed on acid-free paper.

08 09 10 11 12   10 9 8 7 6 5 4 3 2 1

Acquisitions Editor:	Cathy Hernandez
Editorial Assistant:	Ena Rosen
Production Editor:	Libby Larson
Copy Editor:	Mary L. Tederstrom
Typesetter:	C&M Digitals (P) Ltd.
Proofreader:	Taryn Bigelow
Indexer:	Rick Hurd
Cover Designer:	Monique Hahn
Graphic Designer:	Lisa Miller

Contents

Preface

Every teacher needs to know about instructional planning in literacy with the brain in mind! This book provides an essential collection of brain-friendly tools for enhancing literacy in the standards-based curriculum and increasing student achievement. Practical tools and strategies to actively engage the diverse learners in your classrooms are featured and the focus is on literacy—a critical area that will not decline in importance.

Here you will find valuable techniques and strategies for increasing student engagement. These strategies get results! These tools have been classroom-tested and can be used with students of multiple ages and varied stages of development. Add them to your own tool kit of great ideas. My hope is that they validate and enhance what you already do effectively.

This "brain book" is designed to

- make literacy and content come alive by offering interactive activities
- provide relevant, brain-friendly, and immediately applicable strategies
- enhance your skill integration and implementation
- ignite your students' natural love for learning
- translate brain research into practical and powerful practices so you can teach with the brain in mind

This book balances cutting-edge brain research and literacy theory with more than 100 specific strategies that teachers can use immediately to optimize learning in their classrooms. You will learn brain-friendly approaches to lesson planning in literacy across the content areas and innovative ideas for curriculum development. Try these effective strategies, watch your students' enthusiasm and test scores rise, and increase your own teacher satisfaction.

The format of this book is very practical and user friendly. It is 90 percent action steps and practical strategies and 10 percent background and theory. Activities are easy to integrate in your program and ready to use. Strategies are geared toward the elementary level but are adaptable to varied age groups—including those in primary and secondary levels. You can use these tools to transform your classroom into a place of inquiry, discovery, and accomplishment!

A challenging and enriching literacy curriculum will stimulate your students' brains, increase their motivation, and boost their literacy comprehension. The materials in this volume represent a "palette of possibilities."

Remember that you are the artist and need to add your own unique brush-strokes to create your personal masterpiece of meaning and motivation in your classroom.

TEXT TOUR

Chapter 1 (Brain-Based Literacy Learning) presents the "building blocks" of brain-based teaching.

Chapter 2 (Activate to Educate!) presents structures to engage student's thinking before instruction.

Chapter 3 (What Does a Brain-Compatible Classroom Look Like?) discusses the importance of flexible grouping structures and provides lots of ideas for independent, paired, and small-group work. Included are multiple ideas for learning centers.

Chapter 4 (Literacy Is *Not* a Spectator Sport!) discusses multiple strategies to enhance the meaning-making process and boost reading comprehension.

Chapter 5 (Differentiate to Motivate!) provides strategies to differentiate the content, process, and product to meet the diverse needs of your learners.

Chapter 6 (Into, Through, and Beyond Boosters) presents practices to initiate, captivate, and sustain active learning throughout all of your lessons.

STATEMENT OF PURPOSE

This book is designed to be of practical and immediate use to you in your classroom or school. The topics are arranged in order according to a typical sequence for implementation. As with many teaching situations, the lesson plan may be altered depending on the needs of the individual teachers and students.

The material in this volume represents pieces of the complex puzzle of brain-based literacy learning knowledge base. This knowledge base on teaching is rich, practical, and real. Like all categories in professional knowledge bases, there is no one right or best way to accomplish the job; there exists a plethora of possibilities for your instructional palette. Professional practice consists of choosing skillfully from one's repertoire to match students' current circumstances and needs. I hope this book will expand your repertoire and stimulate professional collaboration and collegial conversations to develop good matches for your students.

This book is dedicated to you, the educator. By learning, trying new ideas, accepting the challenge of a new paradigm, and taking a chance on new strategies, we are illustrating for our students that we, as teachers, are lifelong learners. There is no better teacher than a role model. I believe that it is possible to improve student achievement by improving the way in which we teach and the way students learn. Enjoy making these strategies come to life in your classroom!

I am honored to serve as your guide for this journey of brain-based strategies for literacy and that you have selected this book as part of your professional library. It is, therefore, most appropriate that this book is also dedicated to your students—for it is for them that we enter the classroom each day.

Fasten your seat belts and let the journey begin!

PUBLISHER'S ACKNOWLEDGMENTS

Corwin Press gratefully acknowledges the contributions of the following reviewers:

Merilee Sprenger
Adjunct Professor
Aurora University, IL

Mary Amato
Kindergarten Teacher
Lazaro Cardenas Elementary
Chicago, IL

Anne Homza
Literacy Professor
Boston College, MA

About the Author

 **Kathy Perez,** a Professor of Education at Saint Mary's College of California, has more than three decades of teaching experience from the preschool level through graduate school. A frequent presenter and enthusiastic "teacher cheerleader," she offers guidance to both novice and experienced educators. She is an international educational consultant, author, and motivational speaker, specializing in instructional strategies and creative approaches to literacy and professional development. She integrates state-of-the-art methods and research with passion and practical insights from her own classroom experiences.

Kathy has taught in many diverse environments, including Richmond and Oakland, California. She has worked as a general educator, special educator, reading specialist, and curriculum and staff development coordinator. In order to "keep it real" she balances her college courses and her work as a coordinator for the California Beginning Teacher Support and Assessment program by serving as a literacy coach in a San Francisco Bay Area middle school, engaging even the most reluctant learners with brain-friendly techniques.

Kathy works with teachers, administrators, and parents throughout the United States, Canada, Europe, Caribbean, New Zealand, and Australia. For the past three years she has conducted extensive training in Singapore and Hong Kong for the Ministry of Education.

For over 34 years, Kathy has kept the dream of teaching alive. As Thoreau wrote: "Dream . . . go confidently in the direction of your dreams. Live the life you imagined."

Brain-Based Literacy Learning

Pieces of the Puzzle

That reading happens in the brain is obvious. How this actually occurs has been a focus of scientific investigation for more than 100 years. What do we really know about how the brain learns to read? We know that whereas speaking is natural, reading is not. Children do not automatically read. They have to learn how to do it. Have you ever thought about what your brain goes through when you read? Reading in its simplest form is a process of decoding and comprehension. The ultimate goal of reading is for children to become sufficiently fluent to understand what they read. Reading begins when someone unlocks the code of a written language system. However, the neuroscience of reading is much more complex than this simplistic view. Reading is an elaborate process that involves decoding abstract symbols into sounds, then into words that generate meaning.

THE RESEARCH CONNECTION

During the past decade, in particular, we have experienced amazing progress in our understanding of the brain and its impact on reading and comprehension. Never before have neuroscientific studies and classroom instruction been so closely linked. Educators can now refer to carefully designed research studies to determine the most effective ways to teach reading (National Reading Panel, 2000).

What does this evidence tell us? Several studies have found that reading originates in and relies on the brain systems for spoken language. Becoming literate is not a passive act. Language arts skills are best acquired when students are actively engaged in the processes of learning and becoming literate (Blachowicz & Fisher, 2002; National Reading Panel, 2000). The major findings of the National Reading Panel indicate that in order to read, children need to be taught alphabetics (phonemic awareness and phonics), reading fluency, vocabulary, and strategies for reading comprehension. These components of the reading process need to be taught comprehensively, systematically, and explicitly.

Another important question about recent research findings is whether teachers can implement these findings in their classrooms. The connection between theory and practice remains paramount in the minds of educators concerned with the issues of reading and comprehension. Reading is very likely the one area of the school curriculum where neuroscience has made its greatest impact (Shaywitz, 2003). Educators have been well aware of the difficulties involved in learning to read and have long debated the best methods to teach beginning reading. Reading proficiency depends on expert teaching so that the reader learns how to access print accurately and fluently.

Brain researchers have developed new technologies for looking inside the brain and analyzing functions and processes. These technologies fall into two major categories: those that examine brain function and those that focus on brain structure. Different technologies are utilized to look at how the brain works. These procedures can be used to isolate and identify the areas of the brain where distinct levels of activity are occurring. Using these technologies, researchers have been able to determine how different brains function when conducting certain activities, including reading. Some of these discoveries include the following:

Novice readers use different neural pathways while reading than skilled readers.

Individuals with reading difficulties access different brain regions to decode text than proficient readers (Wolfe & Nevilles, 2004).

The brains of people with reading difficulties work harder than those of skilled readers (Devinsky & D'Esposito, 2004).

With proper instructional intervention, the brains of young, struggling readers can be rewired to use different cerebral areas that more closely align with those of typical readers (Bergen & Coscia, 2001).

READING COMPREHENSION AND THE BRAIN

Clearly, we have a lot to learn. Investigators and researchers have worked hard to understand reading and the brain and now have a place to focus their research. The ultimate goal of reading is for children to become sufficiently fluent to understand what they read. Reading comprehension depends heavily on spoken language comprehension. Reading comprehension is a complex cognitive process that relies on several components to be successful. In order to comprehend a printed word, we first need to decode it. However, much more is involved. To develop these comprehension skills, students need to interact with text to derive meaning and develop vocabulary and linguistic knowledge.

The primary area of the brain that has to do with this meaning-making process is the temporal lobe (Wolfe, 2001). The temporal lobes are located on each side of the brain just behind the ears. Looking through this new focus on brain imaging, we can see how some children experience greater challenge and struggle in becoming readers. It is important to look at appropriate interventions for these children. Some students can read and not understand a word, and yet others seem to understand everything but struggle with decoding the words. Because of this discrepancy, educators are vitally interested in information and strategies that are brain based and can assist them in reaching all students and engaging them in the reading process.

Teachers need to use a variety of strategies and techniques to engage the students' brains (Caine & Caine, 1997). In keeping with brain-based theory, applications for instructional practices that are brain compatible have been developed. A sample of the research is offered via the strategies. These strategies also take into consideration how to build the reading brain and how to differentiate instruction. This book offers additional resources to help you to extend and enrich your thinking and to best make sense of the information.

PERSONAL CONNECTIONS

Students are better able to comprehend information when they integrate learning with their own life experiences. "Our brain is most efficient at recalling and using episodic memories that have important personal meanings" (Sylwester, 2000). Therefore, the brain responds best in a learning environment when it can make the connection between the learning going on and real-life applications. The brain is more alert and pays more attention to that learning when it is connected to material that is perceived to be useful in real life. Teachers need to explicitly draw the connection to real life in the classroom. For instance, it is more feasible to introduce a lesson or topic with a demonstration, interactive experience, or case study that shows the relevance of the new topic to real-life concerns. In fact, the more the student is engaged in the process of seeing the meaning and connection of the material presented to their everyday life, the better the opportunity to construct meaning.

Once teachers get to know the students in their classrooms, they need to determine how to present the content in ways that will connect with those students and engage them in the process. Skillful and effective teachers

- Find out what students already know about a topic
- Present the content in a contextual framework
- Decide on a process of delivery that speaks to their particular group of students
- Vary the output of information and the input required by the students

REFLECT TO CONNECT

It is vital that teachers remember the "gum" and "chew" of learning. The "gum" is the content, and the "chew" is the process. We can give our students content, content, content, but if we don't give them time to "chew it over," to reflect and to connect it to their own lives, the learning is not as meaningful as it could be. Therefore, in designing any lesson or content to be covered, teachers need to plan for both the "gum" and the "chew." Reflection and metacognition can greatly aid in the whole effort of finding the patterns and drawing out the meaning of information and events (Caine & Caine, 1997). In other words, the *how* of teaching is just as important as the *what* of teaching. Engaging, metacognitive activities, which on the surface may seem to take time away from learning valuable content, are actually activities that can enhance, enrich, and extend the learning of the material that is being reflected upon to become part of the student's long-term memory system. For some students, it is only when time is allowed for reflection that lasting connections of the material are made.

SLOW DOWN TO GO FASTER

Another way to describe this important process of brain-compatible instruction is to "slow down to go faster." Let's imagine that there is a target in the back of the classroom. That target represents the teaching goals, the standards of the lesson. As the teacher, you have a bow and arrow. The arrow is the "content." You could run to the back of the room with the arrow of "content" in your hand and place the arrow on the target, *or* you could place the arrow into the bow, pull back on the bow, and propel the arrow forward in a much more efficient and effective way to reach the target. Sometimes in our classrooms, it is much more efficient and effective to "slow down to go faster" with our content to assist and support our students in meeting important subject matter standards.

DIFFERENT WAYS OF KNOWING— DIFFERENT WAYS OF SHOWING

Learning occurs in an environment that accommodates and fosters various ways of being intelligent. Dr. Howard Gardner argues that traditional ideas about intelligence employed in educational and psychological arenas for almost 100 years require significant reform (Gardner, 1983). He became concerned about the narrow definitions of intelligence being used by educators and researchers alike. He began to see different intelligence capabilities emerging in different persons. Eventually, Gardner (1999) identified eight intelligences: visual/spatial, logical/mathematical, verbal/linguistic, musical/rhythmic, bodily/kinesthetic, interpersonal/social, intrapersonal/introspective, and naturalistic.

Since Gardner's original listing of the intelligences in *Frames of Mind* (1983), there has been a great deal of discussion as to other possible intelligences for inclusion. Added to the original list of seven intelligences is *naturalistic intelligence.* Naturalistic intelligence enables individuals to recognize, categorize, and draw upon certain features of the environment (Gardner, 1999). Other intelligences explored have been *spiritual intelligence,* which developed into *existential intelligence,* a concern with "ultimate issues" (Gardner, 1999). He also suggests the case for inclusion of *moral intelligence,* although it is difficult to come to any consensual definition of the moral domain (Gardner, 1999).

The impact of these intelligences on classroom practice is obvious. The theory validates educators' everyday experience: students think and learn in many different ways. If teachers are designing lessons for literacy to meet the individual needs of the students, then lessons need to be designed that provide choices and capitalize on the students' strengths. Let's take a closer look at these intelligences and the implications for learning.

> **Visual/spatial**—can picture things visually and enjoys creating products using design and layout skills. Uses maps and other graphic information well.

> **Logical/mathematical**—enjoys abstract thinking. Plays strategic games, easily calculates math problems, and acquires computer skills.

> **Verbal/linguistic**—loves reading and is persuasive and clever with words. Fluid writer, good verbal and auditory memory.

> **Musical/rhythmic**—gathers meaning from music. Can easily hear melodies and rhythm. Moves rhythmically to music.

> **Bodily/kinesthetic**—enjoys activities that involve movement. Good timing and talent in athletics and/or drama. Likes to take things apart and reassemble them.

> **Interpersonal/social**—enjoys performing tasks with others. Can correctly interpret a social situation. Has many friends and is a leader.

> **Intrapersonal/introspective**—can detect and express complex feelings in self and cares deeply about own self. Individualistic, enjoys performing tasks and activities alone.

> **Naturalistic**—good at observing, understanding, and organizing patterns in the natural environment. Shows expertise in the recognition and classification of plants and rocks.

Existential—exhibits the proclivity to pose and ponder questions about life, death, and ultimate realities.

The strategies presented in this book will utilize techniques that tap into all of the intelligences, so that the individual strengths of each student can be supported in the classroom through literacy.

2

Activate to Educate!

What we do immediately before the reading experience may matter as much as the literacy experience itself. This chapter is a collection of brain-based activity structures designed to get students' minds active and engaged, calling into mind prior knowledge about a topic *before* studying it—*activators.*

It is this quality—students getting cognitively active with the reading material—that is responsible for the learning effect of activators. How much the rate and durability of literacy learning is enhanced when teachers regularly use activators is difficult to quantify. However, the shrinking attention span of today's students makes teaching more complex and challenging than ever. The brain research is extensive about the importance of getting students cognitively active with processing information before they begin the literacy learning experience (Harmin, 1995). High-involvement lessons elicit a high level of student engagement. There is solid justification in the research for teachers to utilize as many of the activating techniques as possible and to apply them regularly (Sylwester, 1995; Wolfe, 2001). Active engagement and movement involves more of the student's brain than does passive seatwork (Jensen, 2001). Once you have begun to accumulate a repertoire of these techniques, the challenging part becomes deciding which one or which type to use in which circumstance . . . or how to "match" your choice to specific students, content, or circumstances.

These techniques are enhanced as a result of collegial conversations about the application and implications of these strategies to support literacy learning. This kind of teacher-to-teacher discussion and consultation will prove fruitful and enjoyable. I urge you to study the techniques in this book, try them out, and use grade-level meetings, team meetings, and department collaborative time (as well as informal time) to compare notes and to use one another as consultants for matching decisions on application of these techniques.

WHY ACTIVATE?

Why activate students' current knowledge and thinking prior to literacy instruction?

- The brain organizes information much like a file cabinet. Information is stored and organized based on connections of the new to the known (Saphier & Haley, 1993).
- Students become cognitively engaged and focused on material to be read.
- We surface student misconceptions and create a "need to know."
- Students feel empowered and more confident—*"I already know something"*—approaching the new literacy material.
- We gather information about how we might want to adapt the lesson plan(s) to match student knowledge, learning style, and interest.

PREREADING STRATEGIES

The following strategies will help develop your students' familiarity with text content and structure. Each of these strategies is discussed more fully in the following pages.

Anticipation guide/prediction guide

People Bingo

Windowpane

Graphic organizers

K-W-L

Preview Puzzles

Sticky-note discussion/graffiti board

Story Impressions

Word Splash

Backtrack

Learning Lineup

Voting With Your Feet

Preview Pairs

Sort and Report

Postcard Connections

ANTICIPATION GUIDE/PREDICTION GUIDE

Overview

An anticipation guide (Herber, 1978) is a prereading response theory usually done independently by the student. It contains a series of teacher-generated statements concerning the topic that the students will be reading about. This strategy lends itself to formulate predictions about the text to be encountered, which stimulates comprehension. Students read and either agree or disagree with each statement before reading the text or story. An anticipation guide can be used to activate and assess prior knowledge, to focus reading, and to motivate less proficient readers by familiarizing them with the major ideas of the content to be covered and stimulating their interest. This structure activates the students' knowledge and opinions about a topic, promotes critical thinking, and serves as a guide for the reading. Some of the statements are true and some are false—the "correct" answers are not obvious.

Anticipation guides are designed to create a need to know on the part of the student. The value of the anticipation guide lies primarily in the discussion that takes place after students independently complete the exercise. Students discuss and debate their opinions and then read to get more information. Then they review their responses and decide if their opinions and beliefs have changed as a result of the lesson or their reading, revising them as needed. This strategy sparks lively discussion and provides clear and compelling purposes for reading and responding.

Furthermore, the anticipation guide serves as a motivational tool to boost reading comprehension. Sometimes the statements might challenge the student's preconceived understanding. This process arouses the student's curiosity about the topic and encourages him or her to use the text or lesson to support or refute the statements. This strategy is applicable to all grades and is a powerful tool especially in the upper grades and secondary content areas. Figures 2.1 and 2.2 show examples of an anticipation guide.

Teachers encourage the students to revisit their guides and their responses when the reading or lesson is complete. Students then discuss how their responses have changed or stayed the same, based on the information provided.

Implementation

1. Analyze the material to be read and determine the major ideas that you want the students to focus on in the selection.

2. Determine students' knowledge of these concepts and whether these issues are likely to support or challenge their preconceived ideas.

3. Write these ideas in short, clear declarative statements that may challenge or support the students' thinking about the topic. These statements should address key points, major concepts, and controversial ideas that students will encounter in the selection.

Anticipation Guide

The following anticipation guide is designed to set the stage for learning. Please begin by indicating your response to each statement. You may use the following key: SA for "strongly agree"; A for "agree"; U for "uncertain"; D for "disagree"; and SD for "strongly disagree."

1. It is helpful to put students in learning situations that create doubt, puzzlement, perplexity, contradiction, ambiguity, and cognitive conflict.

2. Reading response theory tells us that meaning comes from the reader and not the text.

3. The single most important activity for building the knowledge required for eventual success in reading is reading aloud to students.

4. Readers, as well as writers, construct meaning as they read and while they write.

5. Readers who might otherwise be considered nonproficient can often demonstrate excellent understanding during literature discussions.

6. The greatest single influence on comprehension is prior knowledge of the subject.

7. Cooperative learning is a teaching strategy where students work collaboratively in structured heterogeneous groups toward a common goal while being held individually accountable.

8. Guessing/predicting strategies really only help proficient readers.

9. Independent silent reading is the major source vocabulary growth, fluent reading, and gains in reading achievement.

10. For new vocabulary and concepts to be learned they need to be related to concepts/vocabulary that are already known.

Figure 2.1   Anticipation Guide

Anticipation Guide

Directions: In the space provided, choose a response from the scale below for each of the statements. Discuss your answers with your partner to see if you can learn anything that will change your responses. After you have finished reading and studying the assignment, take this quiz again and compare your new answers with your original ones.

SD	D	U	A	SA
Strongly Disagree	Disagree	Uncertain	Agree	Strongly Agree

_____ 1. _____

_____

_____ 2. _____

_____

_____ 3. _____

_____

_____ 4. _____

_____

_____ 5. _____

_____

_____ 6. _____

_____

_____ 7. _____

_____

_____ 8. _____

_____

_____ 9. _____

_____

_____ 10. _____

_____

Figure 2.2   Anticipation Guide

4. Put these statements into a format that will elicit anticipation and prediction making.

5. Present the guide to the students and review the directions orally with the class.

6. Have the students complete the guide individually, prior to discussing their responses with a partner or the group.

7. Discuss the statements and have students verify responses. This can be done during a prereading discussion by asking for a hand count of responses to each statement. Call on students from each side of the issue to justify their responses. Encourage students to evaluate their response while listening to the opinions of others. There are two other ways that these opinions can be shared effectively. Please see descriptions of Learning Lineup and Voting With Your Feet later in this chapter. These are excellent structures to use for sharing the anticipation guide.

8. Refrain from telling the students the "correct" answers to the responses prior to reading. This would diminish their need to know and thereby negate any incentive to actually read the text.

9. Assign the text selection. Have students evaluate the statements in light of the author's intent and purpose and/or the information provided in the text. As they read, encourage the students to keep in mind their opinions about the statements as well as the opinions others offer. Have students find evidence that supports or refutes their responses in the anticipation guide.

10. After students finish reading, have students revisit the guide, confirm their original responses, revise them, and participate in a follow-up discussion.

11. Contrast readers' predictions with author's intended meaning.

12. Lead a class discussion of what the students learned from the reading.

PEOPLE BINGO

Overview

People Bingo is an engaging strategy that builds a sense of community in the classroom and enhances oral language development. This strategy, which can be used across the grade levels and content areas, is useful in the prereading stage to generate student interest and personal association with the topic or theme being introduced. As a "people search" technique, it is most effectively used when introducing a new topic or theme.

The activity involves a series of explicit or indirect topic questions on a recording sheet grid to which the students will respond. Each student should be able to respond to each statement with a "yes" or "no" response. This activity promotes student communication and interviewing skills.

It allows students to get to know members of the class in a different way. The purpose of People Bingo is to activate prior knowledge about the experiences being surveyed and creates a need to know on the part of the students. It motivates students to inquire, "What does this question have to do with the topic or reading assignment?" As students move around the room asking questions and gathering autographs for the various responses, their interest in the upcoming topic is escalated.

This structure provides an excellent icebreaker at the beginning of the school year. It is a fun, engaging way for students to get to know one another, to establish a sense of community in the classroom, and to build oral language. Figure 2.3 shows an example of People Bingo.

Find someone who . . .

Can list five countries of Africa Name _____	Can determine which country in Africa has the most valuable resources Name _____	Can compare the population of South Africa with that of Morocco Name _____
Can locate the highest mountain in Africa Name _____	Can tell you a fact they find interesting about Africa Name _____	Can name at least five animals you might see on a safari in Africa Name _____

Figure 2.3   People Bingo Example

Implementation

1. Review the unit of study, chapter text, or novel to be introduced. People Bingo can be used in any curricular setting and content area.

2. Develop statements or questions that support the selected topic or theme. These connections can be direct or indirect.

3. Prepare People Bingo grid sheets. The number of boxes depends on the age and ability level of the students, and the topic chosen. The questions or statements should be clearly stated.

4. Distribute grid sheets to students to begin activity. Model the process for struggling readers by displaying the grid on a transparency and reading the statements aloud.

5. Be sure to encourage the students to get a different signature for each box in the grid.

6. Invite students to move around the room and interview their classmates for the information contained on the response grid.

7. Record the student responses on an overhead or chart paper. Discuss the responses and have students make predictions about the content of the upcoming unit of study or textbook to be read. Compare and contrast their ideas and responses. Have them revisit their predictions throughout the unit, text, or story.

WINDOWPANE

Overview

This is an interactive technique that begins with a quick-write activity in which the student is asked to respond to four open-ended prompts. These prompts are each placed in a quadrant of a sheet of paper that resembles a "windowpane" in the graphic design. This structure is designed to invite the students to activate their background knowledge about the topic and to respond appropriately. Teachers should model the activity first by reproducing the windowpane on an overhead transparency. Divergent responses are encouraged. After a finite amount of time (two to three minutes), students can share their responses with an Elbow Partner (adjacent partner), Learning Lineup (p. 31), or Clock Buddies (p. 58). Figure 2.4 shows an example of a windowpane activity.

Implementation

1. Review the unit of study, chapter text, or novel to be introduced. Think of some issues or responses that could be generated by the issues or themes in the unit.

2. Develop statements or questions that support the selected topic or theme. These connections can be direct or indirect. The statements can be factual or personal. You can have the students reply in words or pictures to the prompts.

3. Prepare the windowpane. Model this activity using an overhead transparency and inviting preliminary responses.

4. Distribute windowpane sheets to students to begin activity.

5. Give the students a brief amount of time to generate their responses independently and silently.

6. After time is called, students can share with partners or table teams or by using a Learning Lineup.

7. Discuss student responses and make predictions about the content of the upcoming unit of study or textbook to be read. Record the student responses on an overhead or chart paper.

Brain-Based Teaching

I think it is . . .

A symbol for it might be . . .

It's important because . . .

I meet the needs of my students . . .

I need to know . . .

Figure 2.4   Brain-Based Teaching

GRAPHIC ORGANIZERS

Overview

Graphic organizers are brain-based templates for learning. These "cookie-cutter" tools come in many sizes and shapes for different purposes. Graphic organizers are visual representations that provide a means of structuring information and allow the students to show the interrelatedness of various topics or to arrange characteristics or qualities of a concept. Not only are graphic organizers important tools to use in the prereading process, but they are also used to increase comprehension during and after the reading process.

As a prewriting tool, graphic organizers can be used to foster discussion and note taking. There are many forms of graphic organizers, including story maps, concept maps, Venn diagrams, semantic organizers, word webs, cause-and-effect charts, fishbone charts, double-entry journals, and cyclical flow charts. They can be used effectively with both fictional and expository texts. As a summary or synthesis tool, they allow for an overview of information in an abbreviated way. Graphic organizers are excellent for visual learners and students who think graphically rather than in a linear fashion. It is important to specifically teach the process and procedures of utilizing these tools with your students. Figures 2.5, 2.6, and 2.7 show examples of graphic organizers.

Implementation

1. Determine the topic or concept that you want to explore with students through visual representation. Graphic organizers can be used in a variety of ways across all content areas. If planning to use a specific tool, teachers need to establish relevant content topics, subcategories, and specific details.

2. Select which structure of graphic organizer will best convey the information needed. Once the topic has been determined, ask, "Which graphic organizer best fits the focus?" and "How can my students best present and record the information in graphic form?"

3. Describe the concept of graphic organizer by discussing
   - The importance of organizing information
   - Various ways people organize information
   - The benefit of using a visual organizer

4. Introduce a specific graphic organizer by describing the
   - Purpose (e.g., a Venn diagram for depicting comparisons). Have students help create categories they are going to compare and contrast.
   - Form and structure (e.g., overlapping circles)

5. Demonstrate filling out the diagram/graphic/map and model the thinking process required to fill out the diagram (think aloud). Modeling the process is critical to student success. Have students follow along, and then discuss in pairs and as a class.

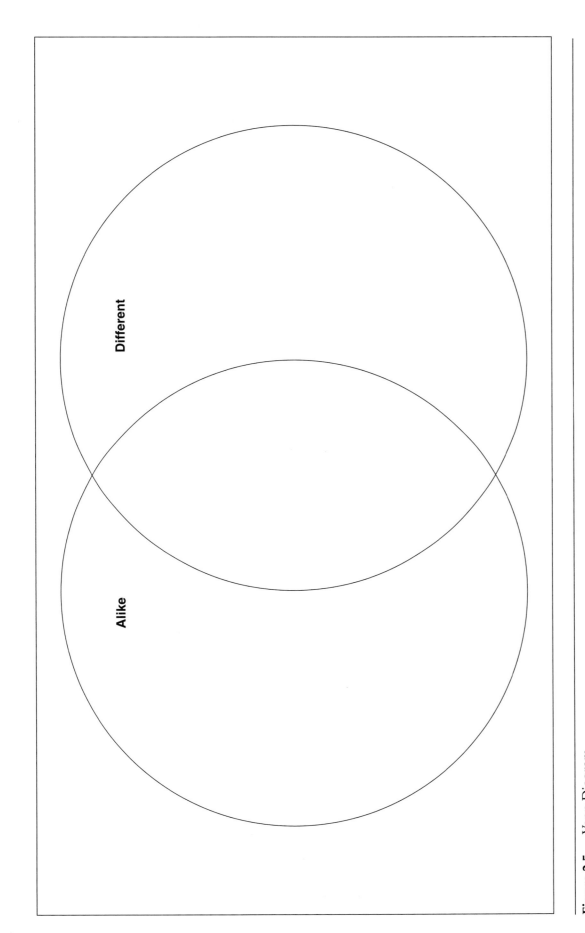

Figure 2.5   Venn Diagram

17

18

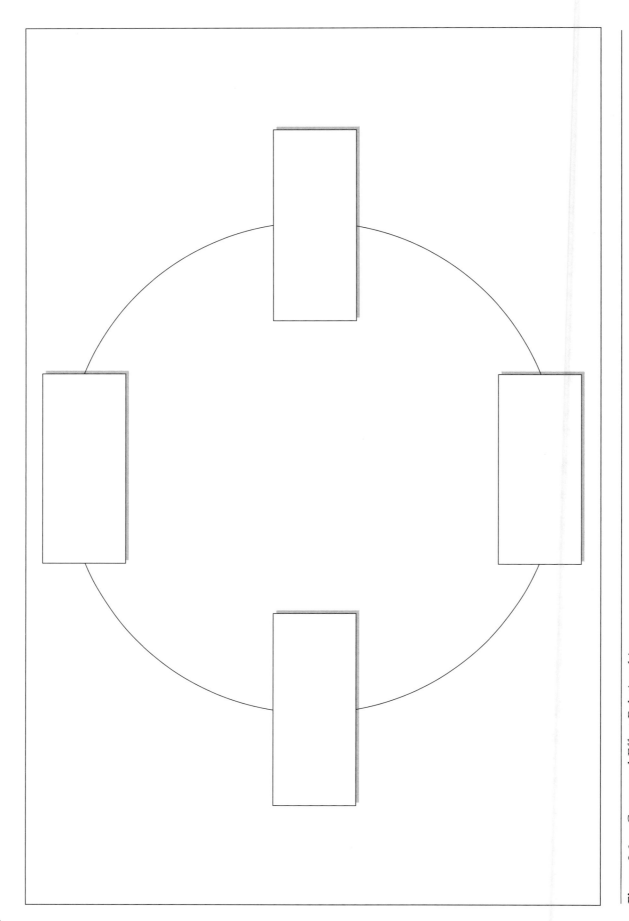

Figure 2.6   Cause-and-Effect Relationships

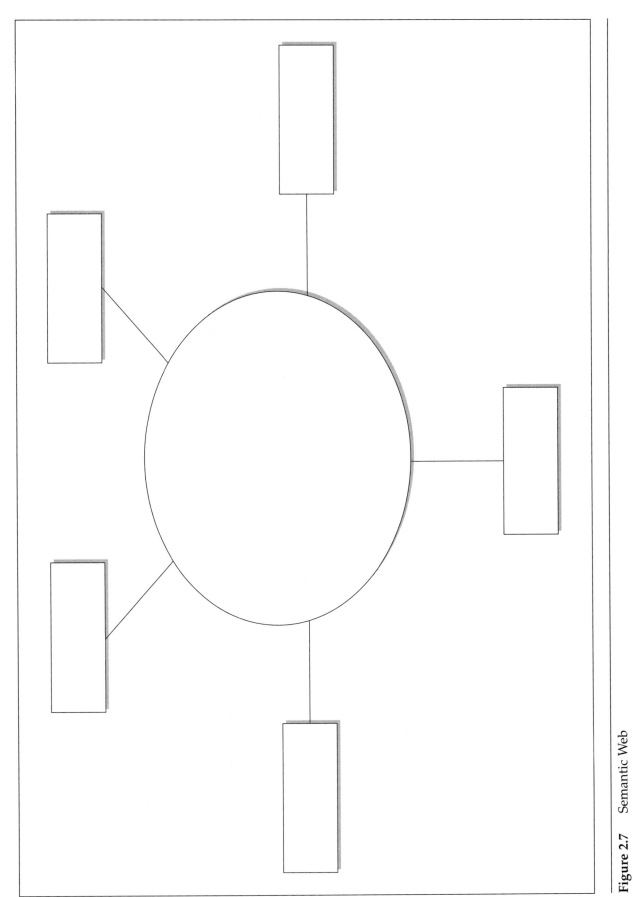

Figure 2.7 Semantic Web

19

6. As you are modeling, explain and demonstrate the use of the selected graphic organizer with
   - Familiar information (tapping background knowledge)
   - New information

7. Next, assign the reading required to complete the organizer and engage the students in gathering and supplying data. Explain how the type of diagram fits the information in the text (e.g., categorical, comparative, representational).

8. To use graphic organizers when lecturing, provide blank graphic organizers and have the students complete them during the lecture. Teacher-student dialogue during the lecture will facilitate this process.

9. As an alternative, complete part of the diagram while students follow along. Then have students complete the rest of the diagram using the text or other materials. This is done in pairs, groups, or individually, followed by class discussion, feedback, and writing prompts. Many teachers like to circulate and troubleshoot while students are completing the organizers.

10. Have students reflect on the use of the graphic organizer by
    - Sharing student examples
    - Evaluating the effectiveness of the organizer according to the established purpose

11. Evaluate the results for missing elements or details—the graphic organizer is not an end in itself. It is a tool to provide information in visual form, and teachers and students should revisit the information to see if any essential information or details are missing or not sufficiently covered to explain the topic.

12. Provide multiple opportunities for students to practice using the graphic organizer.

13. Encourage students to construct their own graphic organizers based on the chapter/text—students create and fill in their own diagrams working in small groups, pairs, or independently. The class then discusses, compares, and elaborates on their ideas.

Structured Dialogue—The Key to the Successful Use of Organizers

1. Demonstrate clearly the use and value of these visual organizers.

2. Model explicitly the thinking processes involved, including lots of interactive dialogue with students as you fill out the graphic, work together, and think aloud.

3. Develop verbal elaboration by students to enhance comprehension— as they explain the graphic to someone else, they discuss their understanding and compare and contrast difference, and so on.

4. Design evaluation of the key ideas and concepts depicted in the diagram to develop instruction/assessment alignment.

5. Foster validation of the thinking process involved and demonstrated— not just the collection of facts.

6. Provide many opportunities for students to work with one another in a variety of cooperative learning structures (jigsaw, think/pair/ share, teams consult, etc.).

K-W-L

Overview

This is a three-step responding process to use before, during, and after a reading selection. This comprehension and fact-finding strategy is especially applicable to informational texts. This technique was first discussed by Donna Ogle (1986) as a way of helping teachers engage their learners in expository texts. The process includes

K—What do we **K**now about the topic?

W—What do we **W**ant to find out about the topic?

L—What did we **L**earn about the topic?

The K-W-L strategy involves brainstorming, categorizing, classifying, raising questions, guided reading, and then locating, recalling, and recording information to answer the questions raised. This critical thinking process is an active, engaging strategy that can also be used as a prewriting, data collection approach.

Teachers can either read the text material aloud to the class or have the students read the material silently or with learning partners. K-W-L involves a high degree of oral language development and questioning between the teacher and students. After sufficient modeling and practice, students can do K-W-L charts with partners or small groups. Figure 2.8 shows a K-W-L chart.

Implementation

Select the material or topic from which to generate the K-W-L chart. Review the information independently before introducing the lesson.

Prereading Stage

1. Create three columns on the board or overhead labeled "What we know," "What we want to know," and "What we learned."

2. Explain to the students that they will be using a brainstorming technique to help them to think about everything they know about a topic.

K What do we already know?	W What do we want to know?	L What have we learned?

Figure 2.8   K-W-L

3. Prompt students with pictures, categories, or subjects and ask "What do you know about . . . ?" Record their responses in the "K" column.

4. Ask the students if there are ways to categorize their responses. If the students put their responses on sticky notes, these can easily be rearranged into categories. You may also want to code the items that fit into certain categories with numbers, letters, or colors.

5. Now ask the students what they want to learn about the topic to be discussed, based on their previous contributions.

6. Record their questions in the "W" column. Leave space for answers when writing responses in the "W" column. In this way, the students can do questions and answers in a summary paragraph after the reading.

7. Explain that these questions serve as their purposes for reading and will help them focus on the important information in the text.

During Reading Stage

1. Instruct the students to read the selection, using the purpose-setting questions as their guide.

2. Please note: Even though this example involves reading a text, this K-W-L structure can be used just as effectively with narrative stories, projects, experiments, field trips, and so on.

After Reading Stage

1. Have the students brainstorm what they recall from the text and write their contributions on the board or on an overhead transparency.

2. Work with the students to answer the questions posed, and verify the statements in the "K" column.

3. After the students have answered as many questions as possible, have them contribute any additional information that they gained on the topic as a result of the reading or lesson.

4. Record their responses and attempt to place them in categories— you may need to create new categories.

K-W-L-Plus Ideas

1. Ask for questions about "What we still need to learn" and record on a "+L" column.

2. Send out student "research teams" to answer the questions raised and left unanswered. This is an excellent strategy for the library/ research connection.

Writing Connections

1. Help the students come up with ways to categorize the information listed in the "What I learned and still need to know." Model a few examples.

2. Another option to try is to have the class or small groups organize the information into a semantic map or concept map.

3. Have students work with learning partners to write about one or more of these categories.

4. Model the process by doing a think-aloud with the class to develop a sample paragraph.

PREVIEW PUZZLES

Overview

Preview Puzzles help build comprehension by giving students an opportunity to understand how a text is constructed and how the parts relate to one another. This hands-on technique uses many brain-compatible strategies. Using informational or narrative text, students arrange sentences or paragraphs that have been duplicated and mixed up. Working with learning partners, they discuss the order that they think makes sense and then put the sentences or paragraphs in that order. The key to this strategy is for students to discuss the rationale they use to determine the order and not to focus just on "getting it right."

Students need to pay attention to transitional phrases and target words in the text that provide clues to the order. They also need to pay attention to the big ideas and supporting details in determining the order. This is an excellent prereading strategy because it ensures that the students will read the text and then carefully reread it to determine the correct order. This strategy, like others in this book, works on the content of the lesson as well as the process of learning it. Students' writing abilities will also be strengthened as they are given opportunities to think and reason as writers.

Implementation

1. Preparation for this strategy is quite simple. Begin by putting the sentences (or paragraphs) from a text or story in random, mixed-up order. Then you make copies of this text for students to work with. Ask the students if the order of the sentences makes sense to them. Why not?

2. Tell the students that the purpose of this lesson is to rearrange the order so that the selection makes sense. Brainstorm with the students the clues they would look for in putting the selection in order. Discuss the use of transition words and certain pronouns that can be helpful in this process.

3. Have the students work with a learning partner and begin to cut the strips apart so that they can physically rearrange them to form a more cohesive whole. Using learning partners is important so that students can discuss their strategies and help each other's thinking. Stress to the students how important it is to pay attention to the strategies they use to do this.

4. Encourage the students as they are working to move the sentences or paragraphs around several times until the passage makes sense.

5. After they have completed their ordering, have each learning pair get together with another pair of students to compare and contrast their arrangements. Ask them to explain their rationale and the clues that they used from the text or story.

6. As a whole class, discuss students' rationale for the order they chose. List the transition words or phrases that provided clues. In addition, list other reasons for ordering that they found helpful. Keep the list posted to provide visual memory for future text passages.

7. Encourage the students to use these transition words and phrases in their own writing.

This Preview Puzzle strategy can be used as an activity in a learning center as students prepare passages on their own for other students to rearrange.

The focus of this lesson is for the students to discuss the reasons behind the way they ordered the sentences or paragraphs. This will assist them in reading informational texts on their own as they begin to recognize organizational devices and signal words. Another benefit of this strategy is that it allows students to integrate these transition words in their own writing.

STICKY-NOTE DISCUSSION/ GRAFFITI BOARD

Overview

This is an active brainstorming strategy that involves your entire class in the discussion of a particular topic or issue related to your course of study or unit. With typical brainstorming in class—the same hands go up, and the same kids say, "Whew! At least she did not call on me!" There is minimal active participation by the whole class. With a sticky-note discussion, you pose a question to the class and everyone needs to respond on their sticky note. They can respond with a word, a phrase, or even a picture. That is why this strategy is so powerful as an inclusionary technique. Each student has an equal opportunity to contribute his or her opinions or ideas about a topic in a nonthreatening way. The sticky notes are anonymous, so they do not need to be concerned about spelling or if they got "the right answer." It is a powerful way to build background knowledge about a topic or to check for understanding. There is little preparation involved, and the results are amazing in terms of ideas generated in a short period of time.

Implementation

1. Begin by selecting a topic or an open-ended prompt or question to pose to the students. For example, you could ask: "What do you know about the Civil War?" Write this prompt or question on a sheet of chart paper or on the white board. This will become the Graffiti Board where all of the responses will be harvested. Give the students adequate think time.

2. Have students jot down their response to the prompt on their individual sticky note. This response can be in the form of a word, phrase, or picture.

3. Ask the students to share their responses with a learning partner (see Clock Buddies, described in Chapter 3). Have them voice their opinions and share their knowledge about the topic.

4. After the students have had adequate time to discuss their individual and paired responses, designate one of the partners to place both of the sticky notes on the Graffiti Board.

5. Review the multiple responses on the board and talk about common themes that emerge. You can ask the students how to categorize these responses. This helps build their critical thinking skills of analysis and synthesis. Invite the students to take a "gallery walk" to view all of the individual responses at recess or the break to learn more.

As an activator activity, this technique provides an excellent way to build, extend, and enrich the student's background knowledge about a topic as they share their responses with others and view the responses of the entire class. It provides an opportunity for them to be more focused on the topic to be taught and sets a purpose for their learning. From a teacher's perspective, this strategy is an excellent way to do a needs assessment on what the students know about a topic or issue before teaching.

As a summarizer technique, students are asked to reflect on the topic or unit that was taught. Provide them with a prompt or a question related to the topic. They write down their response on a sticky note as before. After sharing their ideas with learning partners and posting their notes on the Graffiti Board, the teacher has an opportunity to assess the level of understanding of all of the students.

STORY IMPRESSIONS

Overview

This active prereading strategy reinforces students' vocabulary knowledge and ability to make purposeful predictions, boosts comprehension, and enhances writing performance.

Story Impressions (McGinley & Denner, 1987) is used at the beginning of a lesson. The teacher selects key words or phrases from the passage to be read. This technique can be used with narrative or expository text. These words are presented in the exact order that they appear in the text or story. Students then write a paragraph using the words in the same order. In this way they predict what the text is about and create their own summary about the text that they are about to read. With narrative stories, students use these key words to predict the story line before reading, using their knowledge of how stories are constructed.

This strategy is used to

- Assess students' background knowledge of a topic
- Activate students' prior knowledge of a topic
- Create a need to know by having students predict what the text will be saying
- Promote active learning
- Help students determine importance and summarize
- Verbalize their learning in writing

Implementation

1. Begin by selecting a text, article, or story that the students will be reading. Identify important terms or key phrases related to significant information or plot events. In selecting the words or phrases, make sure that they represent the action, theme, or main concept of the chapter or story.

2. List the words in the order in which they appear in the text or story. This step provides the students with clues to the sequence of events or cause-and-effect relationships in the story. Model this strategy first as a group, displaying the words on the overhead.

3. Make a student worksheet with the words in order, connected by arrows, so that they understand the sequence.

4. Read the words and phrases to the students. Clarify any concepts that they do not understand. Encourage the students to create a picture in their heads to help them visualize the concepts, connections, events, and characters. Students can work on their own or with learning partners to generate connections for the words on the list.

5. Ask students to use these key words and phrases in order to create a possible version of the text or to predict a possible story line. Students create a paragraph representing their prediction of the text. Make sure they use all of the terms and phrases in the word chain.

6. Circulate among the learning partners or teams to provide assistance and support participation.

7. Provide time for students to share with the class their predicted possible version of the text or story.

8. Have the students read the text, paying particular attention to the key words and phrases introduced, and compare it to their summaries. For a narrative story, have them compare the key phrases and how they contributed to the plot. As they read, students will check off the words in the chain that they used accurately in their summaries. Students should discuss and clarify the words and phrases with the information in the text or story.

9. Have students rewrite their summaries based on the new information they gained from reading the text or story. Compare their initial summaries with the rewritten summaries.

10. An extended application of this strategy would be to use it to prepare for an essay exam. Students are asked to summarize their learning by linking the key phrases together into a meaningful synthesis of their learning.

11. Students can also prepare word chains for one another as a comprehension activity to prepare for a new lesson.

WORD SPLASH

Overview

Word Splash is a creative, engaging way to introduce key vocabulary to your students. Modified from the "Word Storm Strategy" (Klemp, 1994) and similar to Story Impressions, this active prereading strategy not only reinforces students' vocabulary knowledge and ability to make purposeful predictions but also serves as a technique to boost comprehension and enhance writing performance. Most terms selected for Word Splash should be somewhat familiar to the students.

For a Word Splash lesson, the teacher selects key terms or concepts from a chapter in a text, an article, or a story to be read. The terms represent important ideas that the teacher wants the students to focus on as they read the passage later. This technique can be used with narrative or expository text. Unlike Story Impressions, the words are presented randomly and at angles, like they are "splashed" on the page. Word order is not important. The novelty of the words and their association with the new topic helps to foster curiosity about the passage to be read and allows the students to make purposeful predictions.

This strategy is used to

- Assess students' background knowledge of a topic
- Promote active learning

Students are instructed to use all of the words to make connections and make complete sentences that demonstrate the relationship between each term.

Implementation

1. Begin by selecting a text, article, or story that the students will be reading. Identify important terms or key phrases related to significant information or plot events.

2. List the words in random order at angles so that they appear to be "splashed" on the page. Model the strategy first on an overhead for the entire class. Most words selected for a Word Splash should be familiar to the students. If not, review the words and their meanings first.

3. Make a student worksheet for distribution, or display the words on an overhead or a chart.

4. Have students make predictive statements about how each of the terms relates to the title of the passage or main topic of the reading. Students can work on their own or with learning partners to generate connections between the words on the list.

5. Ask students to brainstorm these key words and phrases and generate complete sentences that clearly show the relationship between each word or phrase and the broader topic. Students draft their own sentences using all of these words and phrases. Teacher can circulate among the learning partners or teams to provide assistance and support participation.

6. Provide time for students to share with the class the sentences that they have created utilizing the key terms.

7. After the students have developed statements for each term, have them predict what the text or story will be about.

8. Have the students read the text, paying particular attention to the key words and phrases of the Word Splash. They then go on a "word hunt" and highlight the key words and phrases.

9. Students then reread the text or passage to check the accuracy of their predictive sentences. Students should discuss and clarify the words and phrases with the information in the text or story.

10. Have students rewrite their sentences based on the new information they gained from reading the text or story. Compare their initial sentences with the rewritten statements.

11. When students have revised their predictions, encourage them to make their own Word Splash and quiz each other.

Variations

- Create a Picture Splash and ask the students to create statements about the pictures and their predictions about the topic.

- As a summarizer technique, after reading a passage have students create their own Word Splash of what they consider to be the key terms.
- Develop a Word Splash related to a video the students are about to see. They should make their statements and predictions prior to viewing. Pause the video at intervals so that students can revise their predictions and discuss their statements.

BACKTRACK

Overview

Backtrack is a prediction technique that enhances comprehension and creates a need to know for the students. Taking a text tour and a picture walk involves starting from the front of the book. The Backtrack strategy starts from the *back* of the book. Without showing the cover, the teacher reads the last few pages of the book, and the students predict what occurred previously in the text.

This strategy helps build the students' critical thinking skills. When they know the end of the story, they need to fit the pieces of the puzzle together to predict the events that set the stage for this ending.

Implementation

1. Begin by selecting a story that the students will be reading. Preview the story and decide at which juncture you will begin the reading.

2. Cover the book jacket so that the students will not see the title or the picture on the front of the book.

3. Discuss with the students the story elements of plot, character, setting, problem, and solution. Talk with them about story sequencing, identifying what happens at the beginning, the middle, and the end of the story.

4. Tell the students that you will be reading the exciting conclusion of a story. They are to listen carefully and then work with a learning partner to predict the events that led up to this conclusion. Proceed to read the last portion of the story.

5. Have students make their predictions about the elements of the story that preceded this conclusion. Discuss their predictions. You may want to chart them as a visual memory tool to refer to later.

6. Read the story from beginning to end, pausing to make predictions throughout.

7. Look at the chart of their predictions. Ask the students the strategies that they used to make those predictions.

8. Have students try it on their own. Have them read the conclusion of a story to their learning partner, and have them make predictions before you read the rest of the book to them.

LEARNING LINEUP

Overview

Learning Lineup is an active strategy that can be used with any age group and any content area. It is a fast-paced, brain-compatible inclusionary strategy that is low risk and high energy. After the students have completed some kind of quick-write activity (see Windowpane or Anticipation Guide sections in this chapter), they form two parallel lines, facing each other, so that each student is directly across from a partner. The teacher provides the prompt and sets up the procedures and routines to be followed. There is a rapid exchange of information between the partners, and the teacher times the responses accordingly. One line moves down after every exchange and the partners keep changing after each response.

There are many ways that you can use a Learning Lineup. This strategy can be an activator before a lesson occurs so that students exchange their knowledge and opinions about a topic. It can also be modified as a summarizer after a lesson so that students share what they know about a topic or remember about a lesson.

Learning Lineups can be used for a variety of purposes:

- To learn respect for individual opinions
- To enhance team building
- To facilitate communication skills
- To promote deeper understanding
- To develop concepts and background knowledge

This strategy provides all students with a positive way to preview or review topics and share information. As with many other brain-compatible techniques, it provides for lots of oral language, encourages students to see one another as sources of wisdom, and provides for essential student-student interaction.

Implementation

1. Begin by selecting a topic that the students will be discussing. It is helpful if the students have had some think time prior to the lineup in order to formulate their opinions or background knowledge about the topic.

2. Have students prepare their responses in writing and take their written responses to the lineup. Some structures that facilitate this communication would include the anticipation guide and the Windowpane strategy. For primary students, the teacher could provide the prompt orally instead of in writing.

3. Stress to the students that the Learning Lineup is not about "getting the right answer." It is about sharing their opinions and beliefs about a topic or a question. In this way, it is a very inclusionary activity. They are only responding to one learning partner at a time, and they boost their own background knowledge about the topic as they listen to their partner's response.

4. Direct students to line up in two parallel lines, facing each other. Each one should be directly across from another student and close enough to be able to easily discuss issues.

5. Designate one line as the "movers" and the other line is the "shakers." The "movers" move to the right one partner after each question is responded to. The student at the top of the line moves to the bottom of the line so that he or she has a partner each time. The student who begins at the end of the line proceeds to the top of the line rapidly. The "shakers" just shake in place while this is happening. Partners greet each other with each move.

6. Begin by giving a prompt and a time limit. For example: "You have 60 seconds to share your opinion about . . ." The discussion then starts. Each partner is given 30 seconds to respond. The teacher provides an auditory signal (bell, chime, train whistle), and the line shifts to connect new partners. The discussion continues. It is crucial to keep the time limits brief so that students stay on track and focused on the topic.

7. At the end of the session, lead a discussion with the students about how their responses compared with their partners. Were there any differences of opinions? What happened? What did they learn?

Variations: Consultation Lineup and Inside-Outside Circles

This strategy can be modified to form a Consultation Lineup. The Consultation Lineup technique is similar to Learning Lineup except that the students are sitting instead of standing. The procedures follow:

1. Students sit in rows A and B facing a partner.

2. Partner A shares his or her opinion or response. Student B brainstorms ideas, solutions (one to two minutes). Partner A records them.

3. Row A moves one person to the left (like musical chairs) so that new partners are formed when the teacher gives the signal.

4. Reverse roles. This time Partner B shares his or her issue or opinion on the topic. Partner A brainstorms ideas, and Partner B records them.

5. Repeat the process and reverse roles with partners several times.

Another variation of this strategy is Inside-Outside Circles (Stone & Kagan, 1994). In this version, students form two concentric circles and rotate around to discuss the topic with different partners.

VOTING WITH YOUR FEET

Overview

Voting With Your Feet is an active, kinesthetic strategy that gets your students up and moving as they express their opinions about a particular topic. The name of this strategy does not mean that your students stand on their hands to vote. Instead, they move from one corner of the classroom to another to express their opinions and choice about an issue. This strategy will energize and engage your students. It is a class-building activity that can be used in a variety of ways.

This cooperative learning strategy requires your students to make choices and express their opinions. It is important that you encourage your students to have reasons for their choices and to listen carefully to others with different points of view. In this way, it provides opportunities for students to learn about one another and their preferences and to respect individual differences.

As an activator, this strategy helps students get energized about a topic and interested in learning more about it. For the teacher, it is an excellent needs-assessment process and an opportunity to gather information about the students' prior knowledge and ways of thinking about a topic. Voting With Your Feet can introduce a topic to the class and provide students with an opportunity to discuss issues with others who might agree or disagree with them. As a summarizer, Voting With Your Feet provides an opportunity for students to summarize key points to remember.

This strategy fits well in a brain-compatible differentiated classroom because it gets students of all abilities thinking and doing. Higher-level thinking skills are fostered when a teacher asks a question that has no single right answer. The question becomes an invitation for the students to think and engages their minds to consider alternatives. By inviting them to get out of their seats and move to one side of the room or another, the teacher has engaged the students' bodies as well. Special needs students and English learners benefit from hearing the opinions of others because it builds their oral language, develops their thought processes, and extends their knowledge about a topic.

Implementation

1. Select a topic and then craft statements that allow students to choose "sides" on the topic.

2. Announce the choices. For instance, "Parents should choose what their children watch on television." The choices are usually posted on signs, one in each corner of the room.

3. Students select one of the alternatives and record it on a piece of paper. It is helpful for the students to decide on one of the choices in writing, independently at their desk first, before they move.

4. Tell the students that they should move to one side of the room if they agree with the statement and to the other side if they disagree. You might also include signs for "strongly agree" and "strongly disagree." Students join others in the class who made the same choices that they did.

5. In the corners, give the students a specific time period to do a pair/share about the reasons for making their choice. Students can pair again for further discussion.

6. Then have students do a pair/share with a student at the opposite side of the room with a differing opinion. They share with them the reason they made their selection and listen to the other's opinion. Have the students practice paraphrasing what their peers have shared.

7. Students then return to their seats. A spokesperson from each corner shares reasons with the class. The teacher engages the students in a whole-class discussion about the different options and the reasons each corner was selected.

PREVIEW PAIRS

Overview

Preview Pairs is an active, verbal strategy that develops your students' oral language and background knowledge before studying a new topic. Students work with a learning partner and take turns sharing ideas about a topic. The session is timed, and each partner gets three rounds of equal "air time."

This strategy is a great way to get your students "warmed up" to participate actively in a class discussion. It can also be used as a technique for students to reflect and connect their learning from the day before or from their homework assignment. This way it serves as a bridge to what is coming in today's class. Students are involved in constructing language and listening to the ideas of others. This stimulates thinking and helps students recall knowledge about the topic being discussed.

One of the important things to consider when selecting this strategy is whether or not students are likely to have some familiarity with the topic in order to brainstorm ideas for a few minutes.

Implementation

1. Select a topic that the students will be discussing.

Examples:
Share with your partner everything you know about
- What we talked about and did in class yesterday
- What you learned from last night's homework assignment
- Things that have been in the news
- Ideas that come to mind as you look at this book, chapter, title, and so on

2. Have students pair up—identify who is A and who is B in each pair.

Round 1

A shares—B listens (45 seconds).

Switch.

B shares—A listens (45 seconds).

Switch.

Round 2

A remembers more ideas—B listens (30 seconds).

Switch.

B remembers more ideas—A listens (30 seconds).

Switch.

Round 3

A remembers more ideas—B listens (20 seconds).

Switch.

B remembers more ideas—A listens (20 seconds).

3. Have students process or write the following:
- Things you and your partner shared that you feel are sure to be true or accurate
- Ideas shared that you want to ask about or clarify
- Question(s) you have about the topic

4. Have A and B record the three most interesting things they have learned.

Suggestions, Variations

- Choose a topic that is comfortable and familiar to students when first introducing this strategy to get them used to this structure, brainstorming, and the pacing of the process. Some suggested warm-ups might include the following: Tell your partner about your house, what you would find in a mall, movies you have seen recently, favorite songs, and so forth.

- Remind students that this is a brainstorming activity and to let the ideas flow freely.
- Adjust the timing of the rounds to match the dynamics of the class and their knowledge about the topic.
- Preview Pairs can be used as an activator (as described) or a summarizer (to review what the students found most interesting).
- Circulate during the discussion to be sure that students stay on topic and to get a sense of the kinds of ideas generated.

SORT AND REPORT

Overview

Sort and Report is an active, hands-on strategy that taps into your students' background knowledge about a topic and creates a need to know. The teacher creates a set of cards prior to learning. The cards contain ideas, terms, pictures, examples, and/or ideas that are associated with a topic or a unit of study. Students work (usually in pairs or small groups) to sort the cards into groups or categories of ideas and concepts that go together.

After the cards are sorted, students create labels for their categories and prepare to explain or defend why and how each item in a cluster belongs in that group. Sort and Report works well with topics where there are clear connections between concepts, terms, pictures, examples, and ideas.

The purpose of this activator is to begin to familiarize students with concepts, words, and ideas that they will be learning about and to gather some information about the prior knowledge and experiences that the students bring to the subject. Figure 2.9 shows an example of Sort and Report cards.

Implementation

1. Select a topic that the students will be learning. List words and phrases that are associated with that topic.

2. Have students work with a learning partner. Ask students to cut the words and phrases into "word chips."

3. Ask students to talk about the words and concepts, sort them into categories, and label each category.

4. Next have students make a prediction about what the reading, text, or article will be about based on the word chips and concepts.

5. Have the students read the passage and then revisit their word sort categories.

Social Studies Lesson (History of Brazil)

German	sausages	language
million	religion	Munich
Spain	civil war	Carnival
20,000	immigration	Brazil
Europe	Civil War	Catholicism
supply	government	Japan
workers	immigration	influenced
native	slavery	Southerners
Africans	descend	celebration

Figure 2.9   Sort and Report Example

6. Ask the students to determine if they need new categories based on this new knowledge. Students are given an opportunity to re-sort based on what they learned in the chapter or lesson.

7. Have students create and record a final sort. Have them give a written reason for the categories they selected.

Variation: Student-Generated Sort and Report

1. In learning pairs, have students generate words or phrases that come to mind when they think of the particular topic or subject that you will be studying.

2. Have the students cut the words or phrases into strips or word chips.

3. Have the students work with their table group or another pair and
   - Share their words
   - Eliminate duplicates
   - Sort their word chips into categories
   - Label each category

4. Select a reporter for each table. That student stays at the table. The other students serve as "roving reporters" and visit other tables and study their ideas and categories.

5. Groups return to their original tables, refine, and add new ideas.

6. Group prepares for discussion by generating discoveries, insights, and questions.

7. Ask students: "As you generated, sorted, categorized, labeled, and visited others to focus your understanding, what did you notice about your thinking and learning?"

POSTCARD CONNECTIONS

Overview

Postcard Connections provides your students with multiple opportunities to think divergently and to connect what they are learning to a visual image. As an activator, the collection of cards can be placed throughout the room at the various table teams. Postcards promote visual literacy skills, provide an interesting "brain break" in your lesson, and also can be used to develop oral and written language skills.

The first thing you need to do is to start collecting postcards. Have your family and friends—and even your students—save them for you. Postcards are great because they are inexpensive, easy to collect, come in all shapes and sizes and fit into any suitcase easily. I recommend going to flea markets, bookstores, record stores, art museums, and tourist shops for the most interesting cards. You can also recycle your old greeting cards by just cutting off the front image and discarding the verse portion.

Once you have your collection, the learning opportunities are endless!

Implementation

1. Postcard Connections can be used as a terrific introductory activity. Place an assortment of cards on the tables. Provide a prompt to the students and have them discuss the cards and select one card that they can agree on that best symbolizes a given topic.

2. Then invite the reporters from each table to discuss and share how that card symbolizes the topic that you are studying. They can even write about it. This activity provides a nice icebreaker and gets your students thinking in new and different ways.

Dominoes

Each student gets three to six postcards. The facilitator or team leader starts by putting one postcard on the floor. He or she tells the group to start connecting the postcards domino style based on any relationship they can come up with. Students keep building this web of images and cards silently until all cards are connected. Then they take time to discuss how/why cards are connected. This is an inclusionary activity because there are no right or wrong answers, and the discussion should not be limited to preconceived notions. This activity works well with students of varying language abilities because the main activity does not involve speaking or writing.

Small-Group Activity

The facilitator/teacher selects four to six cards at random and gives them to small groups (three to four people). The task of the groups is to make connections and to explain to the whole class how and/or why they are connected. This activity does assume that students have the ability to discuss their choices. The small-group configuration makes it more comfortable for all students.

Individual Responses Within Small Groups

Students sit in teams of four to six people.

Each student gets one postcard and a blank sheet of notebook paper.

Step 1: Each student answers Question 1 in either phrases or sentences based on the card that he or she was given.

Question 1: If you could enter the environment of this image, what sounds (even silence) would you hear?

Step 2: Pass the paper and the card clockwise; each student answers Question 2 based on the new card.

Questions 2a and 2b: What's missing in this picture? What would you add?

Step 3: Pass again and answer Question 3.

Question 3: Think of all the ways we tell time. What time is it in this image?

Step 4: Pass again and answer Question 4.

Question 4: If you were part of this picture, what would you be doing? Why?

Step 5: Pass again if there is a fifth student; if not, your group can just reflect silently for an extra moment.

Question 5: If you were in this picture, where would you be going? Where would you end up?

Step 6: Pass again, returning card and paper to the originator.

Step 7: Write a paragraph incorporating all responses (three to five minutes).

Step 8: Either pass the cards around again so everyone reads all the paragraphs or leave pictures and paragraphs at table; students do a "gallery walk" to circulate and read various responses.

Follow-up question: How did this activity broaden your perspective or change the way you view images? Did you learn anything new about yourself?

3

What Does a Brain-Compatible Classroom Look Like?

By changing your classroom environment, you can deliver more content in a more meaningful way and have your students understand and retain more. In this chapter, we explore specific, brain-compatible enhancements to ensure greater engagement. We also look at various flexible grouping patterns to support learning.

Take a look around your classroom. What do you see? Last year's mellowed and yellowed posters? Stacks of books and papers on shelves full of dust? Faded bulletin boards that have not changed in months? Or do you see a vibrant, print-rich, kid-friendly environment that is invitational to learning? Your students are guests in your classroom. How do you prepare for guests at your home? Strive for an environment that is fresh, alive, and full of vitality!

Your classroom impacts students' ability to focus and retain information. Various seating arrangements support your learning outcomes. What is your classroom environment saying? In this era of standards-based curriculum and tighter teacher accountability we must focus on student engagement. Everything in your classroom sends an important message to the learner—one that propels or detracts them from engagement.

Brain-compatible classrooms are brain-friendly places. These classrooms recognize the uniqueness of each learner and are set up to be safe, stimulating environments. Stimulate students' brains by developing a challenging and enriching curriculum and classroom. Create an inclusive, supportive environment to skyrocket learning. Increase motivation and comprehension with an active learning environment.

TIPS FOR DEVELOPING A BRAIN-COMPATIBLE CLASSROOM

Supportive Environment

Develop personal connections with students.

Create a community of learners in the school through cross-curricular and cross-grade-level activities.

Focus on avoiding threatening situations that interfere with learning.

Provide students with clear expectations and opportunities for risk taking.

Meaningful Content

Establish relevancy for what is to be learned.

Provide real-life, hands-on experiences for learning.

Create opportunities to link new learning with background knowledge.

Choices

Give students chances to take ownership of their learning.

Provide opportunities for students to make choices of books, topics, and projects to display learning that utilizes multiple intelligences.

Timing, Pacing

Provide time for students to reflect on their learning (the "gum" and the "chew") to make connections.

Provide various "state changes" to increase learning, changing the input or output of the information presented.

Provide multiple learning situations for students to immerse them in the information and the application of it. Remember the "10/2" rule—for every 10 minutes of content shared, give them 2 minutes to reflect and connect to it.

Lively Environment

Use props and peripherals to increase the visual impact of the classroom.

Display learning resources throughout the room.

Design learning units that use many modalities and various entry points to learning.

Change materials often—the brain seeks to be continuously challenged, and novelty is important.

Use affirmation posters to reinforce the learning.

Plants and pets can enhance the lively, interactive environment.

Use music to set the mood, change the states, and create a positive learning environment.

Collaborative Atmosphere

Teach and model collaborative and cooperative skills.

The human brain thrives on social communication—provide multiple opportunities for interaction among students.

CONTENT AND PROCESS ("GUM" AND "CHEW")

Most teachers are very well grounded in the content of their instruction. However, the *process* of conveying that information is vital for learning, retention, and transfer. The brain-friendly classroom depends on the teacher's becoming more in tune with every facet of an enriched learning experience. An analogy of this is the "gum" and "chew" of learning discussed in Chapter 1. The "gum" is the content, and the "chew" is the process. Finding creative ways to engage the student in significant learning activities becomes the real challenge for the teacher in today's diverse classrooms. Brain development focuses on engaging the process of learning rather than digesting facts without a specific outcome. Have your students search for meaning rather than just retrieving the answers.

Know the Learners

The primary focus needs to be on the learners. A student-centered focus involves asking yourself these questions:

- Who are they?
- What are their talents and challenges?
- What experiences do they bring?
- What makes them unique?
- What motivates them?

Relate and Motivate

Teachers often make assumptions about which students appear to be "motivated" and which are not. However, these judgments may not always be supported by clear evidence. For example, a student may appear to be "unmotivated" during math class while the teacher discusses rote computation. That very same student may eagerly count the change in his pocket. Effective teachers help students take charge of their learning. In a brain-friendly classroom, students are not merely the passive recipients of knowledge but are constantly shaping their lives as they learn.

Understanding what motivates the student is a key to more successful learning. Some techniques to help teachers find out what motivates students include

- Providing choices and alternatives in assignments
- Speaking informally with the students
- Paying attention to what the students like to write about or read in their spare time

Hands-on, Minds-on Learning

Hands-on experiences help the student understand what is being taught. Different brain structures are engaged by different interactive approaches. Engaging students in discovery can foster critical thinking as it applies to real-life situations. If we teach in a traditional lecture format, we not only limit their learning outcome but also reduce the transfer of learning from the lesson.

It is important to use a variety of strategies to engage the whole mind and the multiple learning pathways. No single instructional technique will maximize the learning of your students. Provide your students with many sources of input, such as books, visuals, stories, videos, drama, discussions, songs, and so forth. Choices in output are also vital to the well-being of the learner: presentations, poems, essays, songs, posters, and so on.

Reflect to Connect

A vital part of the "gum" and "chew" process of learning is providing your students with time to reflect on the content. For many students, it is only when time is allowed for reflection that they make important connections to the material. Constantly just "covering" the materials does not allow students time for processing. Pausing occasionally for reflection is vital for transfer. It is like constantly pouring water into a cup that is already full. Give students frequent breaks in the lessons to better connect with the material. Refer to the "10/2" rule as discussed earlier in this chapter: For every 10 minutes of content, you should provide your students with 2 minutes to reflect and connect before moving on. Students can discuss, write, or reflect upon their learning with this valuable think time. This process enhances the quality of learning and students' subsequent responses.

STATE CHANGES

In a brain-friendly classroom, learning is enhanced through the use of "state changes" (Jensen, 1998). You change the state of the students every 10–12 minutes to boost retention. State changes involve changing the input or the output required of the learning task. By facilitating students' states we can maintain their interest and engagement in the lesson. Since the body and mind are connected, we can move the body to recapture the mind. If we do have students' attention, we have a chance for learning to occur. However, if we just keep "pouring in" the content regardless of their engagement—retention is problematic. To regain or maintain useful states, use "state changers." Some samples of state changes include

- Subdivide the group
- Tell a story
- Role-play
- Stretch break
- Mind maps
- Cross-laterals
- Visualization
- Games, manipulatives
- Teamwork
- Oral affirmations
- Ask questions
- Popcorn ideas
- Repeat after me
- Pair/share
- Discussion
- Partner reteach
- Use of music
- Play "Simon Says"
- Text posters
- Graphic organizers
- Take a deep breath and exhale slowly
- Switch seats to gain a fresh perspective
- Clap three times
- Whisper the answer
- Stand up for the next part of the lesson

Applications

Take a stack of 10 3" × 5" cards and write one favorite "state changer" on each card. Keep them close at hand (on your desk, in the chalk tray). When you notice your students' attention waning, pull out a card and change their state to invigorate.

Here's a tip: Match the state change with your learning outcome. If you are at a reflective time in the lesson, use a simple deep breath or use "outcome sentences." If the tone is livelier, have the students stand and mix and mingle. You need to feel the "pulse" of your group for the appropriate state change. The goal is to facilitate students' states so that they maintain the most optimal frame of mind.

Tune In to the Senses and Emotions

Sensory experiences stimulate input that increases the chance for transfer of learning. New information, when associated with sight, sound, smell, touch, and feelings, is more meaningful and retained for a longer period of time. Similarly, emotions are critical to learning and getting information into memory systems. Many classrooms are passionless and sterile places, as schools have had difficulty understanding the important role of emotions in learning.

Emotions can help us set priorities, achieve goals, and focus on issues that are important. We can engage students' emotions through stories, visuals, videos, and interactive learning. Students can be invited to share their feelings and opinions about a topic instead of worrying about what is the "right" answer. Controversial issues can be debated or expressed in drama or role-plays.

Students are more interested and engaged when they use their emotions and senses because emotional learning has preferential processing in the brain. Emotions play a critical role in the cognitive functioning of the brain. Paying attention to only cognitive activities in the classroom neglects the power of emotions in facilitating learning.

Celebrate Differences

Gardner's work (1983) emphasized the importance of an expanded view of intelligences and different entry points to learning. Multiple intelligences and learning style theories support the fact that students learn, think, and show their work and learning in unique ways. It is important that you use a wide array of different strategies that celebrate the unique talents and strengths of all of your students. It is not only vital to stretch students in different ways of being smart but also important to provide them with multiple assessment opportunities. In this way they can show what they know in various ways.

Furthermore, students' brains develop at different rates. Therefore, multiage practices and flexible grouping patterns support a more developmental perspective to learning.

Assumptions

There are certain assumptions that we need to consider in designing a brain-friendly classroom. These assumptions celebrate the unique learning needs of all of our students and their differing entry points to learning. Some of these basic assumptions include

- Helping all students succeed is essential.
- All students differ as learners.

- All students need appropriate, challenging, supportive, and varied learning experiences.
- Supporting individual needs requires a flexible approach to teaching and grouping.
- Tuning in to student differences needs to be rooted in research-based curriculum and instruction.
- Effective teaching and learning is more than a "bag of tricks"—it is an ever-evolving process.

MANAGEMENT TIPS

- Have a strong understanding of why a brain-friendly classroom is important and convey this to your students and their parents.
- Take it one step at a time—begin at a pace that is right for you.
- Keep in mind the attention span of your students, and design group or independent work accordingly—pacing is critical.
- Use specific "anchor activities" to engage your learners so they experience success and you can focus on meeting individual needs.
- Make sure your directions are clear, succinct, and presented in multiple ways, if necessary.
- Create management signals and processes for your students to work independently while they are waiting for help from you.
- Scaffold increasing responsibility for your students.
- Constantly evaluate your procedures and routines for greater clarity.

GROUPING AND FLOOR PLANS

Answer the following questions to guide your decisions about grouping and space planning.

What is the *purpose* of the activity? What are the possible ways to group, pair, and so on?

How can I incorporate some movement or state change in the lesson to create novelty?

What social or behavioral factors do I need to consider in designing grouping strategies?

What kind of grouping makes the best sense and instructional fit for what we are learning?

What physical boundaries do I have in the classroom? How can I overcome them?

LEARNING CENTERS

Learning centers are an invitation to independent learning. Students are engaged in developing their skills and taking responsibility for their own learning by

- Exploring
- Responding
- Recording
- Constructing
- Practicing
- Applying

Each center should be designed to satisfy three rigorous criteria:

- Independence
- Sustainability
- Meaningfulness

Learning centers and interest centers contain a collection of activities and materials designed to motivate students' exploration of topics and ideas. Centers are designed so that learners interact with materials in order to reinforce concepts and extend their thinking or skills.

An **interest center** is designed to capture the students' interest or passion. These centers often provide enrichment activities that go beyond mastery by engaging learners with meaningful, challenging tasks.

Centers can be designed to reflect the readiness of the students (from simple to more complex tasks), interests of the students, or by considering their learning profiles.

Centers should

- Focus on learning outcomes (standards)
- Utilize multimodalities
- Include differentiated activities that vary from simple to complex and structured to be more open-ended
- Provide clear directions for independent use
- Include options of other activities to do when a task is completed
- Include a record-keeping system to help the teacher monitor progress

Ideas for Assessment and Record Keeping

Response journals

Checklists

Student surveys

Student interviews

Center folders—work samples

Center-specific rubrics

Why Use Centers?

Provides more depth and breadth of content

Student choices

Focused on student interest

Multiple intelligences

Creative applications

Levels of readiness

Promotes independence

How Do We Use Centers?

Focus on learning goals—understanding of concepts or skill development that students need

Provide a level of complexity from simple and concrete to more abstract levels

Provide activities from more structured to open-ended tasks

Develop clear directions as well as specific outcomes

Create sponge or anchor activities for students who finish early

Develop a record-keeping system to monitor what students have accomplished

Coordinate a plan for ongoing assessment to monitor student growth toward learning goals

Provide and plan for necessary materials and resources that students will need in the various centers

SAMPLE CENTERS

Newspaper Center

Students read the daily newspaper and complete various task cards that recognize their varied learning styles.
Sample task cards might include

- Cut out an interesting picture. Write a sentence describing what happened right before this photo was taken.
- Cut out five people pictures from the paper. Write a story about these people and how they might be connected to one another.
- Find an ad in the paper and describe why your family should or should not buy this product.
- Make a collage of words that you find in the paper that describe you.
- Cut out an interesting picture from the paper and write your own news story to explain it.

- List today's weather in five different countries.
- Cut out a photo from the sports section. Write at least 10 different adjectives to describe it.
- Look through the classified ads and pretend that you have $1,000 to spend to furnish your apartment—what would you buy?
- Look through the sports section and cut out 10 action words. Add 10 more action words yourself.
- Rewrite a headline using your own words.

Book Review Center

Students read a book and learn how to write a book review. The teacher compiles book reviews so that other students can read all book reviews in deciding which book to choose.

Poetry Center

- Students read a variety of poetry books.
- They take poems that have been cut into strips and manipulate them on a pocket chart to determine the order of the lines. Then they copy the poem, add an illustration, and keep a collection.
- Students create their own "found poems" by cutting random words from magazines and gluing them on construction paper.

Creation Station

Students write "sticker stories" using various stickers and rubber stamps. They get to read other classmates' stories and work on creative drawing and writing pages.

Write to a Friend Center

At this center, students practice writing friendly letters to their friends in the class using proper letter and envelope form. They deliver these letters to the class mailbox (made out of milk cartons) and also write responses to the letters they receive.

Never-ending Story Center

Students add to a "progressive story," that is, they read what a student has written before and then add the next part or the conclusion to the story. This is a great way to extend and apply story elements including character, plot, setting, and solution. Keep the completed stories in a binder for others to read.

ABC Book Center

For this center you will need to collect several ABC books as examples for the students to peruse. These should be on a variety of subjects to provide the students with ideas. The students then make their own ABC book about a specific subject in the content areas that you are studying. Each student in turn will design a page related to the subject that starts with a specific letter of the alphabet. This may involve research on the part of the students to gather the information needed on a subject to make the book. The students bind and publish their book, and it is added to the class library.

Greeting Card Center

In this center, students create their own greeting cards using "recycled" pictures and images from greeting cards or pictures from magazines. Students need to write and create their own verse. This is a perfect example of "literacy for a purpose."

CREATING INDEPENDENT LEARNERS

In order for centers to be successful, students need to be taught to be independent learners. Some steps to creating independent learners include

- Teach the skill or behavior you want your students to learn
- Organize space and materials to support student ownership and efficacy
- Develop systems for managing movement, behavior, and student needs
- Design activities that are engaging, moderately challenging, and meet the needs of individual students
- Encourage ongoing assessment (self/group)

STRATEGIES FOR FLEXIBLE GROUPING

Students have diverse learning styles and needs and multiple entry points to learning. Flexible grouping is essential for creating a supportive and effective learning environment.

When you think about a brain-friendly classroom, you need to get beyond the "sit and get" syndrome. Teaching to meet individual needs requires a variety of grouping patterns to maximize the learning and the engagement of the students.

Varying grouping strategies better provides for the needs of individual students and enhances student learning opportunities. I like to think in terms of providing a daily "balanced diet" of grouping strategies depending on the content and the outcomes of the lessons. Just as it is important to have a balanced diet to meet our nutritional needs with daily portions of the four basic food groups, it is also important to provide our students with a balanced diet of grouping patterns.

A good way to remember the four basic grouping patterns follows:

T = Total group

A = Alone time

P = Partner work

S = Small group

MANAGING FOR GROUPING ACCOUNTABILITY

Environment for Grouping

Always have directions for work on the board, on an overhead, or in a handout for visual learners.

Have high expectations that students will help one another.

Keep a list of rotating "experts" in the room so that students know they can get help from someone other than you.

Group Accountability

Assign student roles within the group (facilitator, recorder, organizer, timekeeper).

Develop group self-assessment rubrics.

Include processing and outcome statements so groups can note areas of strength and areas in which to grow.

Encourage individual accountability.

Have students assign themselves and their group members part of total score points.

In certain cases, a specialized plan or contract may need to be developed to increase accountability.

Flexible grouping allows students to be more involved in the teaching/learning process—learning not only from their teacher but also from their peers and on their own. Using a variety of grouping strategies can result in improved use of teacher time and classroom materials and enhance students' learning environment.

PLANNING FOR GROUPING

Teachers need to determine how to group students based on the following:

Ability

Preassess for readiness

Kid watch for readiness

Interests

Interest inventories

Class discussions

Personal profiles

How Students Learn Best

Learning styles

Multiple intelligences

Alone, in pairs, or in groups

MIX-MINGLE-SWAP

Overview

Mix-Mingle-Swap is an active, kinesthetic strategy that gets your students up and moving as they express their opinions about a particular topic. This strategy will energize and engage your students. It is a class-building activity that can be used in a variety of ways.

This cooperative learning strategy allows your students to make choices and express their opinions. In this way, it provides opportunities for students to learn about one another's opinions, beliefs, and preferences and to respect individual differences.

As an activator, this strategy helps students get energized about a topic and interested and curious in learning more about it. Mix-Mingle-Swap can introduce a topic to the class and provide students with an opportunity to discuss issues with others who might agree or disagree with them. As a summarizer, Mix-Mingle-Swap provides an opportunity for students to summarize key points to remember.

This strategy fits well into a differentiated classroom that is brain-compatible because it gets students of all abilities thinking and doing. Higher-level thinking skills are fostered when a teacher asks a question that has no single right answer. The question becomes an invitation for the student to think and engages his or her mind to consider alternatives. By inviting students to get out of their seats and move around to music, the teacher has engaged the students' bodies as well. Special needs students and English learners benefit from hearing the opinions of others because it builds their oral language, develops their thought processes, and extends their knowledge about a topic.

Implementation

1. Select a topic that the students will be discussing.

2. Students number off in small groups from 1 to 4. Students jot down their number on a small slip of paper.

3. The teacher begins by playing music and instructing the students to trade their number card as if it were a "hot potato." They keep swapping number cards until the music stops.

4. Students then freeze and look at the number they currently have in their hand. Students are asked to quickly form four groups—that is, groups of individuals holding the same number, and discuss the topic or prompt provided by the teacher.

5. The music starts again, and the fast-paced swapping of the number cards continues. When the music stops, students freeze. This time the teacher asks students to form groups of three or four—with *no* numbers the same. Students discuss the new topic or question provided by the teacher.

6. The music starts again, and the fast-paced swapping of the number cards continues. When the music stops, students again freeze. This time the students form groups of two—odd numbers together and even numbers together with no two numbers the same. Students discuss the question provided.

7. The music starts again, and the fast-paced swapping of the number cards continues. When the music stops, the students freeze. This time students form pairs with 1's working with 2's and 3's working with 4's. Students discuss the question provided.

8. The music continues as students return to their seats. The teacher leads discussion on ideas generated.

CAROUSEL CRUISING

Overview

Carousel Cruising is a structure designed for small groups of students to activate their learning about a particular topic. It works best with a topic that can be divided into a series of subtopics or a series of questions about a topic. Large sheets of chart paper are posted around the room. Each sheet has a different subtopic or question. This active, kinesthetic strategy gets your students up and moving as they share their responses about a particular topic. This strategy will energize and engage your students.

In small groups, students rotate from one chart to the next to brainstorm what they know about each question or subtopic. Each group has a different colored marker to contribute their ideas. Groups "cruise" around to all the charts and return to their original chart to see what other groups have added.

Implementation

1. Write a question or subtopic on each chart.

2. Divide students into small groups. Choose a recorder and a reporter for each group.

3. Give each group a different colored marker and send the group to a chart to start.

4. Direct the students to brainstorm responses to the question or subtopic. The recorder writes the responses on the chart. Give them a specific time period (three to five minutes). Students stop when you give them a signal.

5. Tell recorders to give the marker to another student in the group, and each group rotates one chart to the right.

6. Repeat previous steps.

7. Continue until each group has brainstormed responses to all the topics or questions.

8. Each group "cruises" back to their original chart and reviews what others have contributed.

9. Students can then group the responses into categories or select the three most significant ideas.

10. Groups report out.

Variations

- Each subtopic or question can be put on a clipboard. Have the students pass the clipboard from group to group.
- Students can remain in small table groups; the charts can then "cruise" around the room from group to group.
- For primary grades, charts can be on the floor and students draw pictures for their responses.
- As a summarizer, students can review and reinforce material already studied by listing what they know or by writing questions for the upcoming test.

WALK AND TALK TOUR

Overview

The Walk and Talk Tour is a small-group strategy that is particularly effective when introducing content that contains provocative ideas, important quotes, complex passages, or confusing information. These passages, quotes, and/or ideas are written on individual charts, and students take a walking, talking "tour" from chart to chart as they discuss, interpret, and extend the ideas presented. The purposes of this activity are to create a need to know, set a goal for the learning, and raise curiosity and boost comprehension when the students encounter the same passages or quotes in the text or story they are about to read.

The teacher chooses the passage or quote for posting on the charts. Charts are then mounted around the room and numbered. Small groups of students are formed and are assigned to each chart. Groups spend three to five minutes at each chart where they discuss, interpret, and react to the quote or idea presented. Their reactions can be verbal or in writing. Students then move on to the next chart and repeat the process with a new quote or passage. This process is continued until they have had a chance to visit all of the charts. When they return to their seats, they discuss and summarize their reactions to each passage.

Implementation

1. Write a passage, quotation, statement, or an idea on each chart.

2. Divide students into small groups. Assign each group to a different chart to start their walking, talking tour.

3. Direct the students to brainstorm responses to the quotes or passages. Give them a specific time period (three to five minutes). Provide them with prompts to discuss verbally or in writing. Students stop when you give them a signal.

4. Each group rotates one chart to the right.

5. Repeat previous steps.

6. Continue until each group has brainstormed responses to all the quotations or passages.

7. Groups report out.

Possible Prompts to Use

"This reminds me of . . ."

"I am beginning to wonder . . ."

"I now realize . . ."

"This means . . ."

"Some problems this might cause are . . ."

"I don't agree with . . ."

"I am confused by . . ."

"Advantages/disadvantages of this are . . ."

"This sounds like . . ."

"This looks like . . ."

"One way to interpret this is . . ."

"A question this raises is . . ."

"Causes/effects might be . . ."

"Some problems this might cause are . . ."

"Some consequences of this might be . . ."

Variations

- Before the students take the walking and talking tour, model and suggest ways to react to the charts, quotes, and/or passages.
- Jigsaw tour—if time is limited, form teams that are made up of the same numbers of students as there are charts posted around the room. One student representative from each group goes to the corresponding chart and discusses it and returns to the home group to share what was learned.

NEWSCAST REPORTING

Overview

Newscast Reporting is a cooperative structure designed for pairs of students working together. This strategy develops students' ability to listen to, appreciate, and learn from the ideas of others as they interview each other. Students are paired, given a focus question, and take turns being the newscaster and the one being interviewed. The students then report their information to another broadcast team—forming groups of four. They report what they learned from the interview.

Students need to be reminded that they will be summarizing what their partners talked about. This enhances the quality of listening and engagement during the interview sessions. To prepare for this activity, it is important to model techniques of active listening, paraphrasing, validating, clarifying, questioning, and summarizing when listening to one another.

Implementation

1. The teacher writes a question or series of questions for the interview.

2. Students form partner groups and decide who will be the news-caster and who will be interviewed first.

3. The newscaster interviews his or her partner. Roles are then reversed, and the partner becomes the broadcaster.

4. Student pairs join another pair and report to the small group of four what they shared in the interview.

Activating Examples

What questions do you have about . . . ?

What do you know about . . . ?

What does this remind you of?

Describe your experiences with . . .

What do you predict this chapter will be about?

Checking for Understanding

What did you find interesting about this lesson?

What are you still wondering about?

How will you use or apply what you learned?

What would you like to know more about?

What new questions do you have about this?

What are you beginning to realize?

What did you find most surprising?

What did you find most challenging?

CLOCK BUDDIES

Overview

Clock Buddies is a structure designed to be an efficient and effective process for pairs of students working together. This structure can provide a necessary "brain break" in your lesson as students interact with one another and share their ideas. Clock Buddies is a great way to pair off students for any activity or discussion.

Figure 3.1   Clock Buddies

The good news about Clock Buddies is that once the students have their clock sheet complete, they can keep it and use it all semester long.

Implementation

1. The teacher makes copies of the Clock Buddies sheet (see Figure 3.1) and distributes them to students.

2. Have students stand up and take their Clock Buddies sheet with them. They find other students and make appointments for each time on the clock sheet. Be sure to explain that each time a student makes an appointment at a given time, they must enter their name on the other student's sheet at that same time. The clock times must agree. For instance, if Mike is Ann's 9 o'clock appointment, then Ann needs to have Mike's name at her 9 o'clock time slot.

3. Give the students a finite amount of time to do this. Play lively music in the background to keep the pace up.

4. You now have an instant way to pair up your students. This comes in very handy when a state change or a "brain break" is needed to process the information learned. For instance, after a lesson in science you could tell the students, "Find your 2 o'clock partner and share with them the three main ideas from this chapter."

5. Please note that the time on the Clock Buddies sheet does not have to correspond to the time on the classroom clock. This means that you do not have to extend the school day until midnight or start at 7 o'clock in the morning!

6. For younger students, you might want to take it one time slot at a time for greater understanding. An example of this variation would be: "Students, please find a 1 o'clock partner." Then you proceed to the other time slots around the clock.

Variations

Students could use other structures, including Seasonal Partners, Day and Night Partners, and so on.

GROUPING "ROUNDUP"

Overview

There are multiple ways to use random grouping strategies in your classroom to promote greater interaction and engagement. The key to the success of these grouping strategies involves careful procedures and routines. Always define the parameters of the structure, providing the students with clear outcomes and a specific time limit. Once they are in their groups, give specific directions.

Implementation

There are many different ways to use random grouping in your classroom. Some of these follow:

Color-Coded Buddies

Students are asked to stand and mix and mingle to the music. They are to find a partner that is wearing a similar color to the one they are wearing. Once they find their color-coded partner, they wait for further directions to respond to the lesson.

Address Buddies

Ask students to think of their home address. Then ask them to concentrate on the first digit of their home address (from numbers 1 to 9). They should stand and flash that number with their fingers until they find a group of three to four others with the same first digit. If they have difficulty finding someone that shares the same digit in their address they can go to the "next-door neighbor" for a visit (one digit higher or one digit lower). After address buddies are formed, the teacher gives directions for their discussion.

The Eyes Have It!

This random grouping strategy involves the students mixing and mingling to music around the room. They need to find someone who has the same color of eyes as they do. That student will be their partner.

Deal Me In!

In this grouping strategy, the teacher needs to count how many students are in class that day. She then counts out the corresponding number of cards. For instance, if there are 28 students present, the teacher would pull out seven sets of four cards from the deck and shuffle them. The cards should be dealt to the students facedown. Students find the others who share their number card or face card (e.g., all the 6's work together, all the kings work together, etc.). The teacher then assigns roles based on the suits of the cards. An example of this could be the heart is the facilitator, the diamond is the reporter, the ace is the recorder, and the club is the observer. In this way, not only are the groups randomly formed, but their respective roles in the group are randomly assigned as well. This technique is very fast and efficient.

Stand Up, Hand Up, Pair Up

When the music starts, the students stand up and put one hand straight up in the air. This is a signal that they need a partner. They spot someone else with their hand up. They meet and both of them put their hands down. The final phase is the pair-up phase. They wait for further directions from the teacher.

Comic Strip Groups

This is a fun, interactive way to do random grouping with your students. For small groups, use the daily comics in your newspaper—usually three to four frames each. For larger groups, use the Sunday comics—usually six to eight frames each. Select the comic strips you want and then cut them out into individual frames and mix them up. Count how many students are in class that day and select that many comic frames. Distribute the comic frames to the students. At the signal, students mix and mingle to music and find the other students who share a frame from their comic strip. For instance, all of the "Doonesbury" strips will be a team, and all of the "Peanuts" strips will be another team. Once the students find their matches, ask them to arrange the frames in the correct sequence to tell the story. After that is complete, you give them directions for the activity or lesson. Comic strip frames can be laminated and mounted on construction paper to use multiple times.

Valentine Pairs

Collect and recycle valentines. Have the students find their "valentine matches" to form pairs. A helpful hint is to wait until the day after Valentine's Day and buy the valentines at a deep discount!

Salt and Pepper Pairs

Prepare a list of word pairs that are commonly associated with one another and duplicate the list or write them on cards. Cut them apart and mix them up. Cards are then dealt out to the students. At the signal, they are to mingle around the room and find their "match." These two matches will now form a pair for the pair/share discussion that follows. Some examples of these matches include the following:

salt—pepper	shoes—socks
spaghetti—meatballs	rain—umbrella
knife—fork	wash—dry
coffee—tea	stop—go
bacon—eggs	comb—brush
pencil—paper	aunt—uncle
sweet—sour	you—me
bees—honey	heart—soul
close—open	peanut butter—jelly
moon—sun	table—chairs
cold—hot	sugar—cream

4

Literacy Is *Not* a Spectator Sport!

Do you have any reluctant learners with the following characteristics?

- Has trouble paying attention?
- Seems bored, "tuned out"?
- Doesn't actively participate?
- Does homework sporadically?
- Seems forgetful?
- Often doesn't complete classwork?
- Sometimes acts out, sometimes is silent?
- Is capable of doing the work but seems unmotivated?

If you answered "yes" to one or more of these characteristics, this chapter is for you! If the teacher does all the interacting with the material—guess what? The teacher's—*not* the student's—brain will grow. The classroom hums with activity when the literacy instruction is active and engaging. Students are busy and involved in their learning. We need to get our reluctant learners actively engaged and participating in the literacy process through the following techniques:

Listening

Speaking

Reading

Thinking

Writing

Practicing

Doing . . . **Literacy is *not* a spectator sport!**

Therefore, teachers need a large set of effective participation strategies in their instructional tool kit to ensure that all students are engaged in every lesson. To make information more meaningful to your students, find an experience they've had and "hook" new information to it, or create the experience with them!

This chapter will provide you with more than a dozen different strategies to boost the comprehension process for even your most unmotivated learners. These strategies are designed to tune into multiple learning styles, intelligences, and learning styles. It is important to provide our students with options in the learning process—different ways of knowing and different ways of showing.

"10/2" Rule

Brain research confirms that a student's attention span is about one minute for every year of age (Jensen, 1998; Wolfe, 2001). Use this formula to determine how long your students can actually remain on task:

Age of brain = minutes of focus

Take the average age of your students. That number, plus or minus two, is the appropriate number of minutes you can expect them to focus. So if you have eight-year-olds, provide about eight minutes of content before you provide a pause in the learning to "chew" it over—called a state change or a brain break. A good rule of thumb is the "10/2" rule—for every 10 minutes of content, provide 2 minutes to process. The reason? If we don't have their attention, it is guaranteed they are not going to learn. However, if we do have their attention, we have a chance!

How can we maximize students' attentiveness without burning them out? The brain operates in alternating cycles of activity and rest, fluctuating in a natural pattern. The strategies presented in this chapter will provide you with tools and techniques for those "pauses" and present active, engaging ways for your students to boost their comprehension.

The brain is amazing! It constantly seeks out new challenges, craves stimulation and novelty, and discovers new ways to use its creative abilities. So what happens when the brain perceives the current lesson to be less than challenging? The brain seeks out stimulation. This can be manifested in a variety of ways—getting up out of their seat, talking with a neighbor, passing notes, comical side cracks, and so on. What would class be like if we kept students' brains focused and attentive? We could teach more effectively with increased results!

NOTE TAKING/NOTE MAKING

Overview

For older students, I call these "Note-Taking/Note-Making" strategies, and I keep a poster in the classroom for them to see and choose how they will respond to their learning. They take a sheet of paper and fold it in half. In one column labeled "Note-Taking" they take their notes in traditional form. In the second column, they choose from one of the "Note-Making" strategies to react and respond to their reading in a meaningful way. For students in the primary grades, I also create a poster with picture icons, which relate to responding in creative ways to show what they know.

Sometimes I allow the students to make a choice, and sometimes I might assign one or two ways of responding. These techniques help provide students with a framework that is brain friendly. Reflecting back on the "gum" and "chew" of learning, these brain breaks provide the necessary "chew time" to retain information given. We need to get beyond just coverage of material and move toward lesson mastery. Ask yourself, "What is it I want my students to learn, and how am I going to get them there?"

Note-Taking/Note-Making Strategies

- Summary
    "I Remember"
- Picture This!
    Sketch-to-Stretch
- Rhyme Time!
- Slogans
- Comparison
- Question?
    Question Card Hobby
    Question Card Relay
    Numbered Heads Huddle
    Talking Chips
- Question!
    Jigsaw Book

- Translation
- Alliteration
- Speculation
- Applications
    Graphic Organizers
- Reflection
    Outcome Sentences
    Exit Cards
    Idea Wave
    Y Chart
    The Foggiest Point
    The Five-Minute Paper
    Snowball

SUMMARY STRATEGIES

Summary and synthesis are important processes for students to master in our standards-based era. Most students are able to retell after reading. However, they may have difficulty with summarizing the key ideas instead of the litany of events. The students take notes on their reading on the left-hand side of the page. Give the students a finite amount of time to summarize on the right-hand side of the page what they found most memorable.

Some ideas to support summary include

- Summarize by creating a headline for your notes or a title (in 10 words or less)
- Summarize with a partner
- Summarize in writing
- Summarize by reflecting on the reading and silently thinking about it
- Summarize with the teacher

"I Remember" Strategy

Have the students read only as much as their hands can cover (usually one paragraph) and then share with their partner in their own words one idea that they found memorable. The teacher could also do a read-aloud (only as much as your hand can cover) and have students take turns with a learning partner and share what they found memorable.

PICTURE THIS! STRETCH TO SKETCH

In most classes, we have two kinds of kids: the ones who say, "I can't draw" or the artists who need a "stadium of crayons." This strategy is not about creating great artists—it is about capturing the essence of the learning in graphic form. This provides a brain-friendly way to connect the learning in pictures or images. It is a terrific strategy for our visual learners as well as English learners who are more successful representing their learning in pictorial form.

Invite the students to read only as much as their hand can cover and then pause. Instruct them to sketch a symbol or association of the key idea of the passage. I keep the sketching time to a minimum because this is not about being a great artist—it is all about capturing the essence of their learning in visual form. Therefore, I usually give them only 30 seconds for this phase. I ask them to use only pencil or pen—not colors—because I want them to concentrate on the visual image, not the details or embellishments.

After they have had 30 seconds to capture the meaning of the passage in pictorial form, give them a signal for "pencils down." Students turn to their learning partner and show them their sketch and describe the meaning. They then listen to their partner and view their sketch and the meaning. This boosts comprehension because each of the partners might remember different things and represent it in different ways.

RHYME TIME!

Converting their learning to a rhyme, rhythm, or "rap" helps students remember and retain the information that they have gleaned from the reading. They refer to their notes and then put the key ideas in the form of a "rap" to help them remember key concepts. They share their rhymes, rhythms, or raps with their learning partners and the rest of the class.

SLOGANS

The brain loves to persuade and loves to sell! Think about the current major media slogans that come to mind: "Just do it!" "Got milk?" "I'm lovin' it!" Invite your students to think about their lesson, the text or the story they have just read, and come up with a slogan to help them remember it.

Some examples of slogans that are about brain-based teaching include

"Participate to activate!"

"The brain—just use it!"

"When learning—no brain, no gain"

"Motivation leads to inspiration!"

"Brain-based! Make it fun—get it done!"

"Turn on that neuron!"

"Be cool for school!"

"Move it—you won't lose it!"

COMPARISON

Asking students to make comparisons between what they know or what they have learned and another object or word helps to stretch their mind and fosters divergent thinking. This process is known as *synectics*— bringing together two seemingly different things and making connections and comparisons.

An example of this technique would be to show the students a picture of a chameleon and ask them to compare it to brain-based teaching. "A chameleon is like brain-based teaching because . . ." The students would generate their responses. You can use any photo or picture and have the students relate it to what they are learning. This really helps to secure the information in the brain.

Here are some content-specific examples:

How is a lawn mower like photosynthesis?

Compare what you are learning with something you find in the refrigerator.

Compare what you are learning with something you would find in a toy store.

Compare what you are learning with something you would find in a hardware store.

Variation: Question Card Hobby

This is a questioning strategy that involves comparison. Distribute blank index cards to students. Ask them to put their name and favorite hobby on the card, and then collect them. Put the cards in a special box or basket for future use. Secondary teachers can keep them in separate manila envelopes for each class. After you have given students a reading assignment or delivered a lesson, take a break and pull out a student's card at random. Ask the student to compare what the class is learning with the favorite hobby that he or she listed on the card. An example might be: "Joey, how is the Civil War like playing soccer?" This is an active, engaging technique to involve all students in the questioning process. It is an excellent way to relate what they are learning to their own interests.

QUESTIONING STRATEGIES

Question Card Relay

Ask the students what they know about relays. Generate many responses. Tell them that Question Card Relay has all the characteristics of a relay race: it is fast-paced and involves teamwork, cooperation, and passing things on. Here are the directions for this questioning technique.

1. Have students form groups of four.

2. Provide each student with an envelope containing three index cards.

3. Ask students to think of a question they have about their reading or the lesson that was delivered. Have them write their question related to their reading or content on the outside of the envelope. Ask them to sign their name on the envelope (this ensures that they will have their envelope returned at the end of the relay).

4. When signal is given, students pass their envelope to the student on their right. That student reads the question and responds on a blank card from inside the envelope. He or she answers to the best of his or her ability.

5. Because this is a "race," give the students a finite amount of time to respond to keep up the swift pace. Depending on the age or ability level of your students, give them one to three minutes to respond.

6. Give the signal to pass the envelope. Students sign the card (for accountability), tuck it back in the envelope, and pass it to the student on their right.

7. Students now receive a new envelope from their team and a new question. They open the envelope and reach inside for a new blank card to respond to this new question to the best of their ability.

8. Process continues one more time, and students respond and sign the response to the third question.

9. When signal is given, the envelope with the three responses is returned to sender. Sender reads and reviews responses.

10. Teacher collects envelopes with responses inside. This provides you with an excellent informal assessment tool. You now know the kinds of questions your students have, and you also now know the level of understanding from the respondents.

Another way you can use this technique is to inform students that you will select five questions from their envelopes to include on the quiz tomorrow. This really excites and empowers them—maybe their question will be selected for the quiz!

Numbered Heads Huddle

This structure provides students with an interactive and supportive way to respond to questions. It involves teamwork and sharing and is fast-paced and engaging. Following are the directions:

1. Students number off in teams, 1 through 4.

2. The teacher asks a series of questions, one at a time.

3. Students discuss possible answers to each question for a specified amount of time (about 30–90 seconds, depending on the complexity of the task).

4. The teacher calls a number at random (1–4), and all students with that number raise their hand, ready to respond. The teacher randomly calls on students with the specified number to answer on behalf of their team.

5. Students are encouraged to acknowledge similarities and differences between their team's responses and that of other teams (e.g., "We predicted a very different outcome. Our response was similar to Juan's group.").

6. The teacher continues posing questions and soliciting responses in this manner until the brainstorming or review session is finished.

Talking Chips

Talking Chips is a strategy to foster oral language skills with your students and to involve them in active, engaging discussions. The Talking

Chips strategy ensures that all voices are heard and helps to balance the discussion process. Here is the procedure:

1. Students copy their name or design a simple personal logo on three small pieces of paper ("chips").

2. Group members explore the assigned topic by contributing to the discussion in random order and actively listening to fellow group members.

3. Each time a student makes a contribution to the discussion (e.g., an opinion, an approach), he or she must place a Talking Chip in the center of the table. This provides a visual symbol that they have made a contribution to the discussion.

4. Students need to wait until all members of their team have contributed a Talking Chip before they add an additional response and place an additional chip into the center of the discussion table.

5. After all group members have equitably contributed in random order, they can retrieve their chips to begin another round of responses.

6. Groups have a finite amount of time to explore the assigned topic. At the end of the time period, every group member should have had the chance to contribute at least a set number of ideas.

Jigsaw Book

A Jigsaw Book (developed by Linda Hoyt) provides your students with an excellent tool to interact, teach, and engage one another in meaningful discussions after a lesson or reading has been completed. The Jigsaw Book is a fun way for students to generate questions. See Figure 4.1 for more information about a Jigsaw Book.

Here are the directions:

1. Distribute 9" × 12" construction paper to students (12" × 18" works best for primary students). Each student will also receive two white paper strips (either 2¾" × 9" or 4½" × 12").

2. Fold the large sheet of paper in half.

3. Fold each side in half again to make flaps.

4. With the paper in the shape of a "W," the center fold should point to the ceiling.

5. Fold and crease in fourths.

6. Using scissors, cut through first fold to second fold, so you are making four flaps.

7. Lay it out flat and be sure that the center fold faces up.

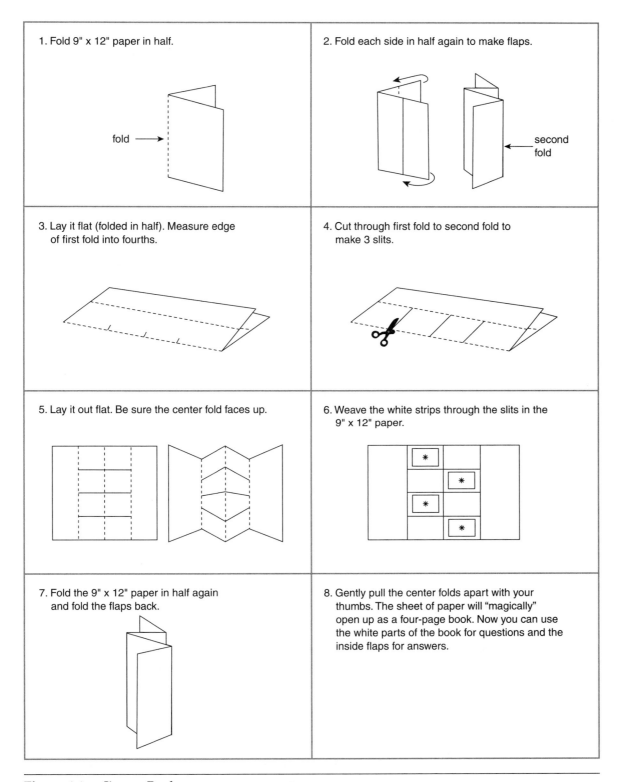

Figure 4.1 Jigsaw Book

Source: Developed by Linda Hoyt. Diagram by Judy Hjelseth. Used with permission.

8. Weave the white strips through the slits in the construction paper.

9. Write a question on each of the four spaces created by the strips.

10. Make paper into a tent and fold the side flaps up again like a "W."

11. Have students say a magic word (e.g., *abracadabra*).

12. Gently pull the center fold apart. It will "magically" open up into a four-page book. Now you can use the white strips for writing and illustrating your answers to the questions.

13. Students swap books and answer questions on a separate sheet of paper.

14. They are able to check and correct their own work, because their learning partner has recorded the correct answers in the Jigsaw Book.

Suggested uses:

- Reviewing for a test
- Vocabulary words/definitions
- Math problems/solutions
- Opposites
- Rhyming words
- Synonyms
- Parts of speech
- Story elements
- Beginning sounds/pictures
- Word problems/solutions
- Foreign words/English translation
- Scientific symbols/meaning

TRANSLATION

We retain about 90 percent of what we teach others, so when we ask our students to "translate" what they have learned or read, retention soars. Translation does not mean translating the content into a different language. Instead, translation implies a shift in language. Here's an example to share: Ask your secondary students to translate the Declaration of Independence in language that a fifth grader could understand. You could also ask your elementary students to translate the story they have read for a first grader. This shift in language not only involves summarizing and simplifying the information but also reinforces the content as they teach each other.

ALLITERATION

In using the technique of alliteration, you invite your students to review their notes, their learning, or their reading and develop an alliterative phrase that will help them remember it. Here are some examples related to brain-based teaching: "Brain-based boosts bountiful bridges to linking learning and literacy" and "Proper practice and preparation prevents poor performance."

SPECULATION

Speculation involves guessing and predicting, and the neurons are in sprinter position to make connections in the brain. Speculation can be used to enhance your students' literacy and create a need to know. There are multiple ways to use speculation to boost comprehension.

Here are some examples:

- As you preview the chapter to be read, ask your students for two important things that they predict they will learn in this lesson or text.
- Pause in a story you are reading to your students and ask, "How do you predict that this story will end?"
- Have your students look at the pictures, the title of the chapter, and the captions in the text and predict the main ideas that will be covered.
- Ask your students to read the questions at the end of the chapter first and predict what the answers will be. Then have them read to validate or refute their speculations.
- Have your students turn the boldface headings in the chapter into questions to be answered.

APPLICATIONS

Graphic Organizers

It is important to utilize various learning styles to help your students into, through, and beyond their reading. Applications are ways to do just that. Applications involve using various learning styles and graphic organizers to help with comprehension and retention. Graphic organizers are like the "cookie cutters" of instruction to help even the most reluctant learners organize their thoughts. The use of graphic organizers is described in Chapter 2.

REFLECTION

Taking time out for reflecting on the lesson is one of the most important aspects of the "gum" and "chew" of learning. Research says that if the teacher spends just three to five minutes on a reflective activity for the lesson, comprehension is increased by 50 percent! So far I have stressed several examples of activators to do at the beginning of a lesson to set the stage for learning. Now we will focus on a few summarizers to assist and support your students' retention of the lesson.

Getting students active in summarizing for themselves what was important, what they have learned, how it is important, and/or how it fits with what they already know are the purposes of reflection. Students often have a difficult time summarizing lesson content, monitoring their understanding and use of new strategies, and reflecting critically on their learning.

Outcome Sentences

This structure encourages students to review a class session and reflect meaningfully on the day's discussion and activities. It also provides the teacher with productive feedback on the impact of the lesson taught.

The teacher provides students with a series of open-ended prompts to reflect on the day's lesson. This can be done verbally by using an "Idea Wave" structure (explained below) or in writing. Possible prompts might include

I now understand . . .

I am beginning to wonder . . .

I was surprised . . .

I can see the connections between . . .

I want to know more about . . .

I would like some help with . . .

I am becoming more confident about . . .

Students write two to three detailed outcome sentences about new insights, observations, or sources of confusion. These can be shared with a learning partner, which could lead to a total class discussion, with the teacher synthesizing and elaborating as appropriate.

Exit Cards

These reflections can also be turned in at the end of the class period in the form of an Exit Card. The teacher meets the students at the door at the end of class, and this is their ticket to leave. This process provides a very enriching form of needs assessment so that you can flick through the cards in a few minutes and determine what students found meaningful and/or what they are confused about.

Students who may feel reticent to seek assistance during class are provided a safe outlet for expressing their needs and concerns.

Idea Wave

1. Students listen while the teacher poses a question, open-ended prompt, or a task.

2. Students are given some think time to consider what they know about the topic and do a quick-write to record a number of possible responses.

3. A volunteer begins the Idea Wave by sharing one idea.

4. The student to the right of the volunteer then shares one idea. Then the next student to the right shares one idea.

5. The teacher directs the flow of the Idea Wave until several different ideas have been shared.

6. The teacher moves the activity around the class in a relatively fast-paced and structured manner, allowing as many students as possible to respond in 15 seconds or less.

7. The students never know where the wave will start or where it will end. That keeps them more engaged in the process and fosters active listening.

8. At the end of the formal Idea Wave, a few volunteers who were not included can contribute an additional idea.

9. The teacher can record these ideas for review or have the students do a quick-write summarizing the contributions of others.

Some Student Pointers for Participation

- Speak only when it is your turn.
- Share only one idea, in 15 seconds or less.
- Respond using a complete sentence.
- Speak loudly and slowly enough for everyone to easily hear your comments.
- Pay careful attention to what your classmates are saying.
- Listen attentively during the discussion.
- Be ready to summarize key points.

Y Chart

Students are provided with a template of the Y Chart with various icons to depict different reactions about the content or topic being studied.

The sample Y Chart (Figure 4.2) has three areas in which to respond. The heart symbolizes "feels like," the ear symbolizes "sounds like," and the eye symbolizes "looks like."

The teacher gives the students a topic or a prompt to consider. An example might be: "What do oceans look like, feel like, sound like?" They can draw pictures or write words in each of the areas. This process helps your students think divergently.

Students prepare individual Y Charts then meet with a learning partner. Students can then meet as teams and compare and contrast their Y Charts and create a team poster to share with the class.

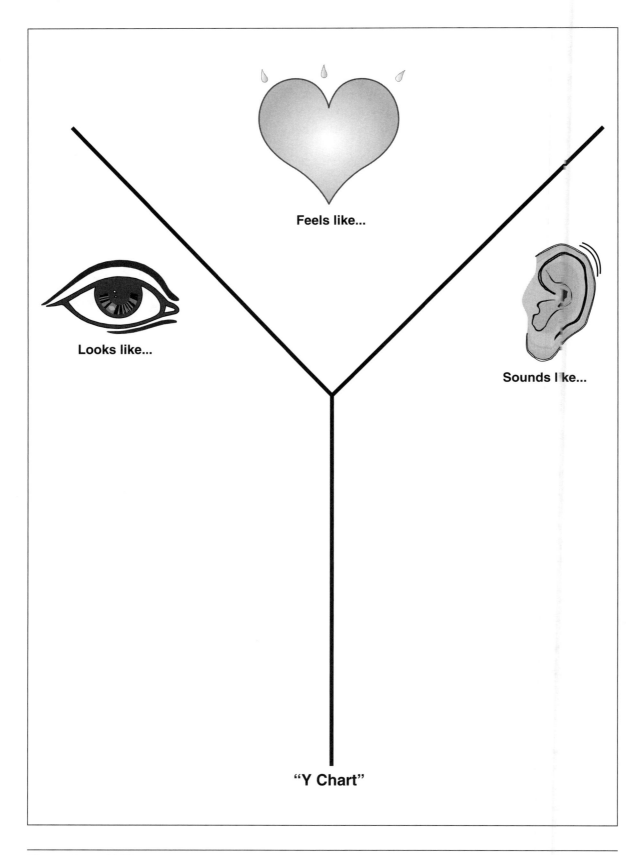

Feels like...

Looks like...

Sounds like...

"Y Chart"

Figure 4.2   Y Chart

This is a powerful strategy for your special needs students as well as your English learners, and it fosters oral language development as well as development of their visual literacy skills.

The Foggiest Point

1. Students are asked to reflect on the lesson, the chapter, and the assignment.

2. They are asked to jot down what the foggiest point in today's lecture, homework assignment, or small-group activity was. In other words, what point was the *least* clear to you?

3. Students spend three to five minutes on a quick-write activity to reflect on their learning and to articulate what they are wondering about.

The Five-Minute Paper

1. Ask the students to reflect on the lesson, the lecture, or the chapter that was covered during class.

2. On a sheet of paper they respond to the question "What were the most useful or meaningful things you learned during this session?"

3. Then they respond to the following: "What questions remain uppermost in your mind as we end this session?"

Snowball

One of my favorite reflective activities is Snowball. It is a fun, interactive strategy that can be used in so many ways.

1. Distribute blank sheets of paper to students.

2. Ask them to reflect on their learning in your class that day.

3. Have them number their papers from 1 to 3.

4. Ask students to jot down three important things they learned in class today.

5. Give them think time and time to jot down their ideas.

6. Ask students to crumple paper up into a ball like a snowball.

7. Have students stand, snowball in hand.

8. Stress the importance of "gently" and "randomly."

9. At the signal, students will gently toss their snowballs in the air and catch somebody else's snowball to find out what was important to them.

Other possible prompts to use:

- Write three new words you learned today.
- Write three successes you had today.
- Write down three new ideas you learned today.
- Write down three questions for homework (whoever catches it will need to write the answers!).

5

Differentiate to Motivate!

What are some simple, low-preparation strategies that will help you to differentiate the content, process, and products of your lessons to meet the diverse needs of your learners? This chapter will focus on specific tools for your instructional tool kit to meet the challenges and opportunities of tuning in to individual needs. Incorporating these strategies into your instructional repertoire will lead to higher achievement for all students.

As teachers map the journey of learning, they must realize that each student travels with a suitcase packed with unique skills, abilities, and interests. Facilitating differentiated learning is not about teaching louder or slower. It is about having an assortment of active, engaging strategies, tools, and techniques to meet the diverse needs of your students. The "one size fits all" approach to teaching and learning is ineffective and even harmful to most students. Students have multiple entry points to learning— "different strokes for different folks." Figure 5.1 reminds us of what students bring to the learning environment.

Differentiation is all about change, challenge, and choice in today's classroom. Change the content! Change the process! Change the product! It is about student readiness, student interests, and student learning profiles. It is about the opportunity to learn in a successful, supportive environment through the many ways of knowing and expressing what one knows. Differentiation is about standards-based learning and high-powered teaching.

Figure 5.1   Our Students Bring . . .

ESSENTIAL ELEMENTS OF DIFFERENTIATION

- Classroom climate of community
- Solid, research-based curriculum
- Continuous assessment that is used to guide instruction
- Flexible grouping
- Multiple instructional strategies

Knowing those pieces of the puzzle, how do we make it happen? What are some strategies for a differentiated classroom?

- Curriculum compacting
- Acceleration
- Learning centers or stations
- Tiered assignments
- Flexible grouping
- Contracts/independent studies
- Simulations
- Writer's workshop
- Reciprocal teaching
- Literature circles
- Open-ended assignments
- Use of technology (tiered software, Web quests)
- Consistent pretesting to find "entry point of learning"
- Decrease total, large-group activities
- Increase small-group teaching activities
- Provide individual alternatives

Students Need a Balance of Both

Traditional teaching styles and practices do not need to be at odds with principles and practices for differentiating instruction. The key is to provide your students with a *balance* of practices to maximize their learning potential.

- Teacher-directed learning—student-centered learning
- Text knowledge—choice
- Test-taking skills—products as assessments
- Teacher feedback—self-assessment
- Standards—constructivist learning
- Individualized—group dynamics
- Following directions—creating plans
- Listening—discussion
- Sequential—multitask

WHAT IS THIS THING CALLED DIFFERENTIATION?

Differentiated Instruction Is Student-Centered

Students come into our classrooms with different levels of background knowledge, interests, and cognitive abilities. Teachers who differentiate instruction seek to provide appropriately challenging learning experiences for all students. Tomlinson (2001) states that "differentiating instruction means 'shaking up' what goes on in the classroom so that students have multiple options for taking in information, making sense of ideas, and expressing what they learn" (p. 1).

Differentiated Instruction Is a Blend of Total Class, Small-Group, Partner, and Individual Instruction

Teachers need to decide which curriculum areas or topics would be most conducive to differentiation. Keep in mind a balance of grouping strategies.

Differentiated Instruction Is More Qualitative Than Quantitative

It is not about the scores, it is about the *quality* of instruction. The "how" of instruction is just as important as the "what" of instruction.

Differentiated Instruction Is Proactive

The teacher proactively plans a variety of ways to accomplish instructional goals. He or she assumes that different learners will have different and unique needs.

Differentiated instruction provides multiple approaches to what students learn (content), how they learn it (process), and how they demonstrate what they've learned (product; Tomlinson, 2001).

Differentiated Instruction Is a Continuous Learning Experience for Students as Well as Teachers

Assessment is ongoing. Teachers make adjustments as needed in content, process, and products.

PIECES OF THE PUZZLE

Preassessment

Profile students' interests, attitudes, experiences, skills, background knowledge, and multiple intelligences through

- Surveys
- Inventories
- Kid watching
- Pretests
- Personal profiles
- Checklists
- Dialogues
- K-W-L

Content

Provide access to the content for all students by

- Tapping into prior knowledge and experiences
- Providing supplemental materials at varying levels of difficulty
- Offering multi-option assignments
- Providing students with choices of assignments, questions, prompts, vocabulary, reading material, graphic organizers, interest centers, and so forth
- Highlighting key concepts and vocabulary
- Creating simplified and/or extension activities
- Using video clips, taped materials, and/or computer programs for simplifying or extending learning

Process/Instructional Methods

Differentiate the method of instruction by utilizing

- Cooperative groups, learning partners, teams
- Flexible, skill-based groupings
- Think-aloud strategies
- Group investigations
- Learning centers
- Learning contracts and independent studies
- Modeling/demonstrating
- Checking for understanding
- Debates
- Field trips
- Guest speakers
- Graphic organizers
- Visuals
- Varied time allotments
- Simulations/role-plays
- Peer and cross-age tutoring
- Multimedia, computers, videos, and taped materials
- Varied instructional strategies such as cooperative learning, synectics, concept attainment, direct instruction, concept formation, and so on

Products/Assessments

Differentiate products by varying, modifying, and/or offering student choice regarding

- Performance tasks
- Work samples
- Quizzes and tests
- Projects
- Oral presentations
- Graphic organizers
- Group and individual projects
- Portfolios
- Self-assessment/reflection
- Evaluate products and assessments using
  o Rubrics
  o Criterion lists
  o Negotiated criteria
  o Varied checklists

MANAGING YOUR DIFFERENTIATED CLASSROOM

First, set the tone for differentiation.

Next, create student profile cards by gathering information about students from

- Academic scores
- Interest inventories
- Learning styles
- Multiple intelligences

Begin at a pace that is right for you—one strategy at a time and one student at a time.

Consider different ways to process learning:
- Walk and talk (walk five giant steps and share)
- Make-a-date clock buddies
- Mapping
- K-W-Ls
- Find someone who . . . (pick a trait, i.e., shoe size, birthday, favorite food)
- Corners (move to corners by traits, interests, or readiness)
- Timed pair share
- Rally robin—form groups of four, go out and learn from other groups, come back and share with your group

Have a strong understanding of *why* differentiated instruction is important and *communicate* your beliefs to your students and their parents.

Keep in mind the attention span of your group—allocate time for group or independent work to be slightly shorter than their attention span. Keep in mind the importance of "brain breaks" and state changes.

Keep in mind "chunk" and "chew"—do whole group activities in small chunks and then let students "chew" or process what they learned in appropriate small-group or individual activities.

Use "anchor activities" to free you to focus your attention on groups or individual students.

Create and deliver clear and careful directions.

Create procedures and routines (a plan) with your students for
  • Getting help while you are busy with another student or group
  • Moving to anchor activities
  • Collecting papers
  • Discussing with learning partners
  • Moving into groups
  • Sharing ideas

Provide your students with as much responsibility for their own learning as possible.

Create three-sided table tents for your students labeled "Hard at Work," "HELP!", and "Finished." (Be sure to check the finished work to see if it is quality work before allowing students to move to anchor activities.)

Utilize parent volunteers to work with small groups and individuals.

Consider peer and cross-age grade-level tutoring.

Appoint classroom managers/resident experts.

Another strategy is to use "Ask three before me." You encourage the students to ask three of their peers for assistance and support before they approach the teacher.

Use metacognitive strategies ("thinking about your thinking") to help students understand your expectations as well as your reasons for those expectations.

Evaluate and refine your procedures and routines.

Always monitor groups by floating and asking questions. Help students troubleshoot. Refrain from giving solutions.

Use Exit Cards or outcome sentences to get feedback from your students as you go through a unit or lesson

Find a partner and collaborate—use team teaching and share your workload.

TEN THINGS TO TRY NEXT WEEK (TO ENCOURAGE INDEPENDENCE AND DIFFERENTIATE INSTRUCTION)

1. Make a list of all the reasons why your students come to you for help. Are they really in need of help, or are they asking you questions about procedures and routines such as "Where do I get . . . ?" or "I'm done. What do I do now?" or "Can I go to the bathroom?" Figure out specific procedures and routines to deal with these issues first and then teach and model them for your students.

2. Teach your students at least two strategies to "unstick" themselves without interrupting you. Some examples include
   - "Ask three before me" (described earlier)
   - Designate a "resident expert"
   - Put name on "help" list and do alternate task until help arrives
   - Put up "stop sign" or other silent signal that you need help and then go to the emergency task card pile to work on while you are waiting

3. Have everyone practice talking to a learning partner or reading to another person using "six-inch voices" so as not to disturb others. Establish a signal to use if voices get too loud and model using it many times.

4. Set a timer for 5 to 10 minutes (depending on the age and ability level of your students) for the students to work independently. They are not allowed to interrupt you. Practice! Start with an activity that the students are familiar with—journal writing or spelling practice, for example. Gradually increase the amount of time by another minute or two until they have demonstrated that they can work independently without you for at least 15 minutes.

5. Teach your students at least two "independent routines" or anchor activities each week. Keep a list of these on a chart on the board. Add a new one to the list each week.

6. Divide the class in half and teach the same lesson twice while one half of the class works on an anchor activity. This way you are engaging the students more fully in small-group instruction while the rest of the class is working on independent study skills.

7. Use a community-building activity such as a Personal Profile and initiate discussion about differences in learning rate, learning style, strengths, and interests. Personal Profiles (Figure 5.2) are graphs that students construct that rate their self-assessment on certain skills at periodic points during the school year. For instance, their profile might indicate on the graph that they are "awesome" in math and maybe "so-so" in spelling.

8. Give the students choices in assignments—different ways of knowing and different ways of showing!

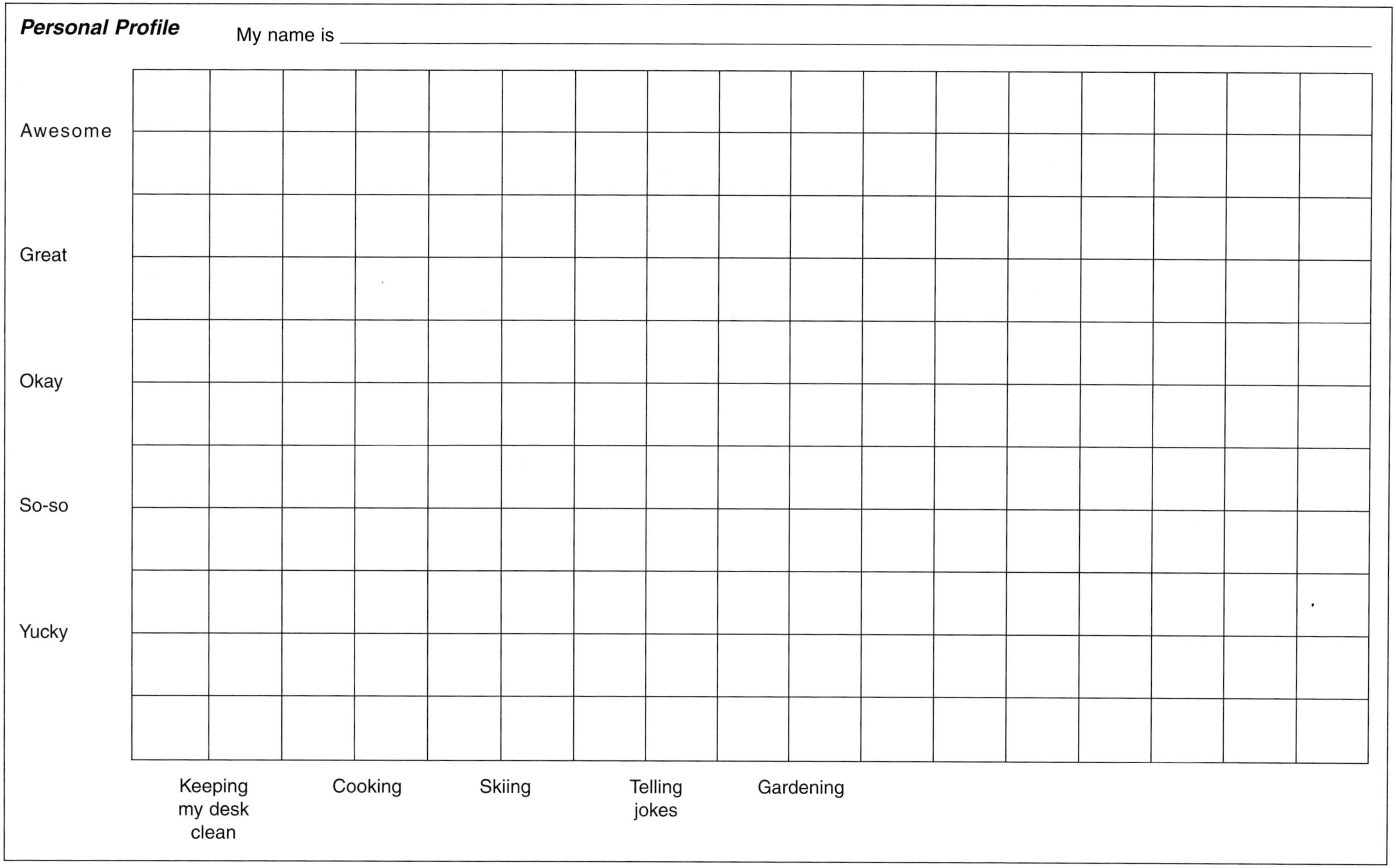

Personal Profile   My name is _____

Awesome

Great

Okay

So-so

Yucky

Keeping my desk clean · Cooking · Skiing · Telling jokes · Gardening

Figure 5.2   Personal Profile

87

9. Use Exit Cards, outcome sentences, or response cards to "check the pulse" of the class at the end of a lesson or at the end of the day, and use the feedback to refine plans for future lessons.

10. Start a "Professor of the Week" program. Each week one or two students are selected to teach other students about something they have an interest in or passion about.

You are a lifelong learner. Begin small, but begin! Differentiated instruction does not have to be a daunting task. Not to begin is a guaranteed way to avoid progress.

LESSON PLANNING FOR ACTION

A typical lesson plan for action and engagement moves at a fast pace. It is organized so that the class proceeds smoothly with high student involvement. Students feel the momentum of the lesson and always have something to do. Pacing and preparation are important. The lesson has plenty of variety and uses multiple instructional strategies depending on the outcomes you want to accomplish.

Here are some questions to ask yourself in planning your lessons to meet the diverse needs of your learners:

- What is the purpose of the lesson?
- How will you know students have achieved this purpose?
- How will you gain and maintain students' attention?
- How will you divide and teach the content to engage students' brains?
- What structures or strategies will you use to deliver the content?

PROFESSOR OF THE WEEK

Overview

This strategy celebrates the unique talents, interests, and knowledge of your students. Each week the selected student or students teach other students about something they have an interest in or passion about.

Implementation

Ask your students, "Have you ever wished you could be the teacher? This is your chance! Each student in my room will become an expert in a subject of your choice, and you will have the opportunity to teach the class about it." This is a unique chance for your students to share their talent with others.

Introduce the concept with some questions: "Do you have an interest in spiders? Does Abraham Lincoln fascinate you? Are you an expert skier? Would you like to learn more about Nebraska? Maybe you have a comic book or stamp collection? Do you know sign language?" The opportunities are endless. The students get to select a topic that they already know about, or they can pick a topic that they'd like to learn more about. It is their choice.

Each student is required to turn in a written report and to use at least three to five reference sources (depending on the age and ability level of your class). Students will be responsible for presenting the information to the class in an oral report. In addition to the written report and oral presentation, students are required to present a visual project. Students can make a poster, shoot a video, sing a song, make a model, do a demonstration, paint a picture, teach a game, and so on.

ACTIVE PARTICIPATION STRATEGIES

Overview

These tools for your engagement tool kit can be used at any grade level and for any subject matter content. They are all brain-friendly strategies that help you differentiate the responses required by your students in an active, engaging way. After all, it is not what you say or do that ultimately matters; what matters is what you get the students to do as a result of what you say and do.

Implementation

Choral Responses

All of your students say it together. This helps to wake up their brain and reinforce important concepts. It gives the students think time. It is very helpful to provide a cue such as holding your hand up. Then drop it to signal it's time to respond. You can also cue the students on the overhead with a pointer to chant together.

Cue students to show you they are ready: for example, "thumbs up when you know"

This works for nonverbal choral responses too: for example, "touch the word" or "put your finger under . . ."

Partner Responses

This is a very powerful strategy to increase active language use, attention, and higher-order thinking during and after instruction.

The teacher chooses partners based on literacy/social skills.

Assign roles A and B. "A's tell B's two things we have learned about . . ."

Specific topic: "What do you predict about . . . ?" or "Share two things you have learned about . . ."

Do it in short, specific time periods to keep the students focused: 28 seconds, 1 minute and 14 seconds, and so on.

Call on students *after* they have practiced with a partner.

The benefits of partner practice before whole class discussions include:

- All students get feedback/clarification/support from their partners
- Students have more time to think and rehearse, encouraging reflection and thoughtfulness
- Students are likely to be more confident and willing to share with the whole group
- An increased number of students are "doing the doing" of learning
- Increased odds that students are attentive/engaged and interested in their peers' responses, comparing/contrasting their ideas with their classmates, and so on
- Teachers get excellent "informal feedback" on their teaching/student needs

Written Responses

This is an important strategy, especially as students move up through the grades.

Writing first increases thinking, accountability, focus, and so forth.

Writing provides the teacher with concrete feedback (e.g., "Do I need to clarify this?").

Written responses connect written language to oral language.

Pictures and graphic representations are welcome.

Independent responses can be turned into team posters to reinforce concepts and enhance a print-rich environment.

Randomly Call on Students

Avoid hand-raising questions ("Who can tell me . . . ?"). If it is worth doing, all students need to be "doing the doing" of learning—not just watching others! This increases accountability, attention, focus, and involvement, and it is more fun, and lively.

One clever technique is to write students' names on Popsicle sticks, place them in a jar, and randomly select them.

Toss Koosh balls or foam Frisbees to students as they respond. This is great for tactile learners and ADHD students, and engages all learners in the discussion.

GIVE ONE/GET ONE

Overview

This structure can be used as an activator to build background knowledge about a topic or as a summarizer to reflect and connect the learning after a lesson. It is an interactive strategy that gets the students up and moving and swapping ideas to boost the comprehension and the meaning-making process of all. Students are asked to generate three ideas about the topic, and their knowledge grows as they exchange those ideas and extend their learning with others.

Implementation

1. Students are given think time to ponder what they know about a particular topic or open-ended prompt that you pose to them.

2. They are asked to record three ideas they know about a given topic. Each student lists three to five ideas related to the assigned topic. They can record this on a grid (Figure 5.3) in three different squares (pictures, words, phrases), or they can make a simple list of words and phrases or series of complete sentences to share with others. If making a list, students draw a line after their final idea to clearly delineate their own ideas from those of their classmates.

3. Students write their name clearly at the top of the page so that their conversation partner can easily read and record it on their sheet.

4. Students are given a set amount of time (about five to seven minutes) to get up and share ideas with classmates.

5. Each student proceeds to give one idea from their list or grid to a learning partner and then add to their own list or grid a new idea from their partner's.

6. After finding a partner, the two students exchange ideas and comment or ask for clarification. It is important that they comment on anything they find confusing or of particular interest because they may be called on to share one new idea during the debriefing session.

7. Students continue interacting and sharing ideas until the specified time is over.

8. When I use this technique I ask that the students exchange no more than one idea with a partner and then move on to another partner for a new idea swap. This keeps the students moving and the ideas flowing.

9. At the end of the Give One/Get One exchange period, the teacher facilitates a unified-class debriefing of ideas. The teacher calls on a volunteer who shares one new idea acquired from a conversation partner, utilizing language for classroom reporting (e.g., "I found out from Michael that . . ." "Susan mentioned that . . .").

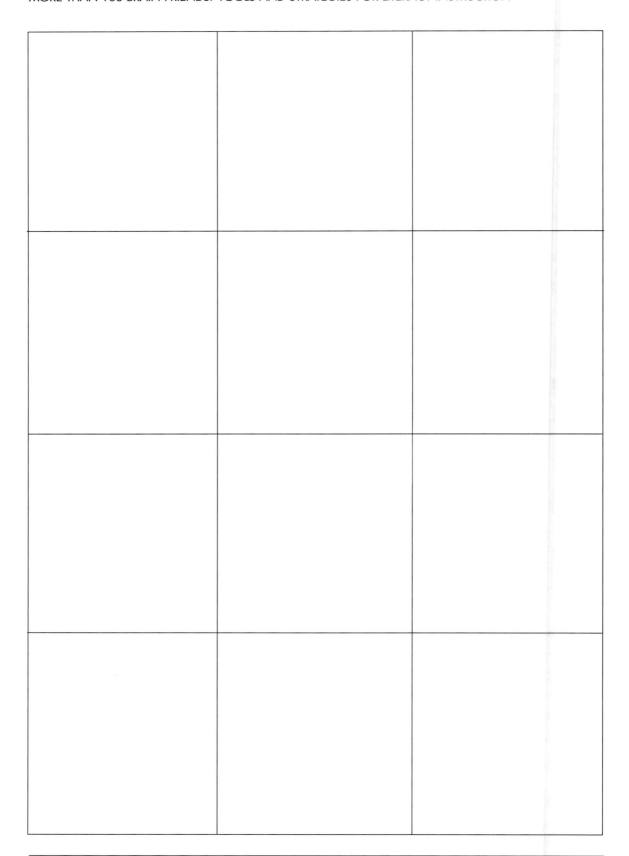

Figure 5.3   Give One/Get One Worksheet

10. The student whose idea has just been reported shares the next idea gleaned from a different conversation partner. This process of structured debriefing continues until a sufficient number of ideas have been generated. This structured debriefing encourages active listening, as students are eager to see when their name and idea will be mentioned.

11. The teacher records the contributions on the board or overhead. This listing can subsequently be restructured in a graphic organizer and used as a springboard for an independent reading or writing task.

SAVE THE LAST WORD FOR ME!

Overview

This structure is an inclusionary activity that boosts listening comprehension and is an engaging way to get the students connected to the text and discussing main ideas together. Students are encouraged to read actively and independently. They then meet in a small group of four for the discussion of memorable points. In this way, everyone contributes, communicates, and validates one another's responses.

Implementation

1. As the students read the passage, text, or story, ask them to put a check mark or sticky note next to five statements that pique their curiosity or evoke a strong response (either positive or negative).

2. After they have finished the reading, they select two of the statements that they found most memorable and write each on the front of a separate 3″ × 5″ card (or fold a piece of notebook paper in half).

3. Underneath the statements, the students write down in their own words what they think the author was trying to say.

4. On the back of each card, students write comments that they would like to share with their group about this statement.

Group Procedures

1. Students number off in groups from 1 to 4 or from 1 to 6, depending on the size of the group.

2. Select a number of your group to go first.

3. Student reads the statement from the front of one of his or her cards but is not allowed to make any other comments.

4. Every other member of the group talks about the statement and shares at least one comment.

5. When everyone else in the group is finished responding, the student who wrote the card can turn it over and read his or her written comments. In other words, this group member has the *last word*!

6. Go on to a second student and repeat the process until all of the cards are shared.

CUBING

Overview

Cubing, developed by Cowan and Cowan (1980), provides the opportunity for students to construct meaning about a specific topic from six different perspectives. We know that different students have different learning preferences. This strategy is a way for you to differentiate the products that you ask the students to create after a lesson. The way you structure questions can either exclude some of your students or invite them into the learning process. Each side of the cube has a different verb, and the students use different thinking processes to complete it. These are all verbs taken from Bloom's Taxonomy and develop higher-order thinking skills.

Some examples might include

- Description: What is it like?
- Comparison: What is it similar to or different from?
- Association: What does it make you think of?
- Analysis: How is it made, or what is it composed of?
- Application: What can you do with it? How is it used?
- Argumentation (Take a stand, arguing for or against it.)

Cubing uses a simple visual and tactile technique to engage your students as they approach a topic from many different angles.

Implementation

1. The teacher models cubing with the class. See Figure 5.4 for a cube template.

2. Students select a topic for writing, or the teacher assigns one.

3. Have students in each group take turns throwing the cube and noting the instructions listed on the part of the cube that lands face up. Students roll the cube and respond accordingly.

   OR

4. Students write for three to five minutes about each of the six sides of the cube:
   - Describe it.
   - Compare it.

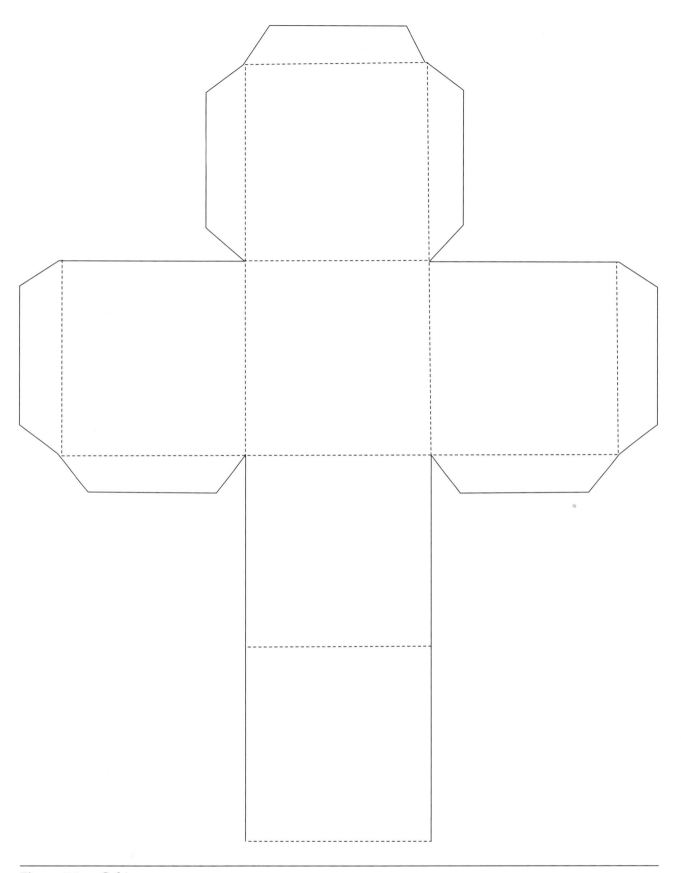

Figure 5.4 Cubing

- Associate it.
- Analyze it.
- Apply it.
- Argue for or against it.

You may need to add specific instructions to the commands to create appropriate tasks for each group. Students use their completed cubes as the springboard for longer writing assignments or for class discussion.

Variation

- You can adapt the designations on each side of the cube to make them more appropriate for your specific content area.
- Students may work in small groups, with each member writing about a different side of the cube, and then combining their work.
- You can color code the cube to differentiate further so that each color represents a different readiness level or to differentiate according to different learning modalities.
- Start with a blank cube pattern and create new cubes that differentiate by student interests.

6

Into, Through, and Beyond Boosters

Developing strategic readers and learners is a complex process. This chapter takes an interactive view of reading and writing to develop your students' mental processes. Reading comprehension—the process of obtaining meaning from print—is fundamental to learning. Checking for understanding after a student reads a passage used to be the way that we tested for reading comprehension. However, research now supports the necessity of setting the stage for comprehension and learning before the students even open a book. It is also important to engage them in the meaning-making process throughout the reading as well as give them time to reflect and connect to what has been read after the reading occurs.

The key concept of this new definition of comprehension is that a reader constructs meaning from a text rather than merely "barking at print" and reproducing the words on the page. Meaning is something that is actively created instead of passively received (Vaughn & Estes, 1986). The more a student knows about a topic, the better he or she will be able to comprehend the printed material on that topic. What sets apart proficient readers from struggling readers? One major difference is that proficient readers reflect and carry on an internal monologue with the text while they read. This ability to "think about thinking" is called metacognition.

A reader's comprehension is also influenced by situations in which the reading occurs. These factors may include physical conditions such as noise or light levels in the room, physical space for the learning, and time elements such as early morning or late night. Teachers have a great deal of influence on the conditions of learning in the classroom. Will the information be discussed the next day or a week later? After the reading, will students take a test, create a poster, or complete a project?

Because comprehension is a result of an interaction of multiple factors, teachers need to pay attention to the reader, the text, and the context for reading. Effective readers utilize various strategies to navigate successfully through this comprehension maze. Proficient readers know how to monitor their understanding: predicting, connecting with prior knowledge, determining importance, self-questioning, clarifying, and summarizing. Classroom strategies that promote the integration and interaction among reader, text, and context are more likely to develop students who can effectively learn from print materials. Some factors to consider are the following:

- Students learn best when they have adequate background knowledge of the topic.
- Frontloading instruction is vital for the meaning-making process.
- Strategies need to encourage students to actively think about what they are reading and to apply what they have learned.
- Teachers need to turn their students from being passive receivers to active constructors of meaning.
- Activities that support students to interact with other students tend to increase motivation and active engagement.
- Students learn best when they become strategic readers.
- Students need to discover which learning strategies best support them and when to apply them.

DEVELOPING AN INSTRUCTIONAL FRAMEWORK

This chapter provides you with an instructional framework to integrate the strategies described in previous chapters. This instructional framework describes which strategies are best suited as activators, as summarizers, or to engage the learner throughout the teaching process. Because many of these strategies have been presented and described in other sections of the book, this chapter provides you with a list of strategies and structures to be used rather as a roadmap and a planning guide.

I have designed this instructional framework for integrating the strategies into your lessons. This roadmap analogy is useful in designing your lessons. Teachers need to present the roadmap (framework) to guide the students in the concepts, skills, and content of the lesson. There needs to be flexibility to accommodate for student differences. The factors to consider in planning your lessons include activating prior knowledge, tuning in to various learning styles, creating a need to know, and maintaining engagement throughout the lesson. You need to recognize that the learning journey may include alternative routes, detours, and resting places depending on the unique needs of your learners. As both teachers and students travel along the learning journey, they have the opportunity to pause, reflect, and connect the learning using these various strategies for engagement.

The phases of utilizing these strategies include initiating the learning, interacting with the materials, constructing meaning, processing the information, utilizing and organizing the content, and then reflecting on it. Reflecting provides students with an opportunity to integrate all aspects of the learning process. Once you choose your target, move ahead to create your own tool kit of strategies for meeting that target.

"INTO" STRATEGIES

Overview

These activities are designed to activate prior knowledge, build background, and set the stage for comprehension. Some of the strategies that are best suited to activating prior knowledge before reading include

- K-W-L (described in Chapter 2)
- Tapping prior knowledge through questioning
- Brainstorming
- Quick-writes
- Teacher read-alouds
- Video clips
- Text tours, picture walks
- Sticky-note discussion (described in Chapter 2)
- Mapping
- Focus questions ("Have you ever . . . ?" "What if . . . ?")
- Anticipation guide (described in Chapter 2)
- Preview Pairs (described in Chapter 2)
- Sort and Report (described in Chapter 2)
- Postcard Connections (described in Chapter 2)
- Field trips
- Interviews
- Research projects
- Speakers
- Dramatizations
- Music or art of the period
- Short story or poem to introduce topic
- Small-group/whole-class discussion
- Word Splash (described in Chapter 2)

"THROUGH" STRATEGIES

Overview

These activities are designed to engage the student throughout the reading and help them make connections to text. Some of these strategies include

- Paired/buddy reading
- "I Remember" (described in Chapter 4)
- Teacher read-alouds (to highlight specific ideas)
- Graphic organizers (described in Chapter 4)
- Think-Pair-Share
- Insert/coding strategy
- VIP strategy (very important point)
- Clock Buddies (described in Chapter 3)
- Learning log
- Reader's theater
- Dramatization/improvisation
- Storyboard
- Student-generated questions
- "Sketch-to-stretch" (described in Chapter 4)
- Speculation (described in Chapter 4)
- Paraphrase
- Comparison/contrast (Venn diagram; described in Chapter 4)
- Personal response
- Small-group/whole-class discussion

CODING STRATEGY

Overview

The coding marking system is an active reading strategy to engage your students and facilitate their interaction with text. It is a particularly helpful way for less-skilled readers to become more aware of breakdowns in comprehension so that they can remember to clarify the issue at a later time. This is most effective when students have their own books or copies of articles and stories and can mark in them. However, students can use sticky notes, separate sheets of paper, strips of paper in the margins, and so forth to deal with a common-use, nonconsumable textbook.

Implementation

1. *Overview and purpose.* Describe the coding strategy and how it can be helpful to use it.

   Coding Marking System

   X   I think differently

   +   New and different information

   !   WOW

   ?   I don't get it

   *   Very important to remember

2. *Demonstrate—model.* Use think-aloud strategies as you model the coding strategy.

3. *Guide class in using coding.* As a whole class, practice using coding. Be sure to discuss your thinking/rationale for using different codes.

4. *Practice in pairs and/or teams.* Structure cooperative pairs/teams to read segments together and use coding. Compare and contrast their marks.

5. *Practice on your own.* Assign homework and/or other independent work using coding (be sure to discuss after, using pairs/teams/ whole class).

Variation: VIP Strategy (Very Important Points)

The VIP strategy is a simple technique that helps your student locate and label main ideas and assists their connection with text. Provide each student with a large sticky note (3″ × 3″) that has been cut into three to four strips with the "sticky" portion intact.

Instruct the students to read the passage, story, and text and to flag the three to four "very important points" with the sticky-note strips. Each student works with a learning partner and shares his or her VIPs and listens to his or her partner's. Students need to support their main ideas and are given the opportunity to change their minds based on the ideas shared by their partner.

Now they are better prepared to participate in a small- or large-group discussion. Students have identified their main ideas and are ready to justify them.

"BEYOND" STRATEGIES

Overview

After the students complete the reading, they are asked to reflect and connect to their learning. These strategies provide the students an opportunity to show what they know in diverse ways. In some structures, they are asked to critique, analyze, and compare. In other techniques, students have an opportunity to demonstrate their learning utilizing many different learning styles and different products. Some examples include

- Learning logs
- Learning Lineups (described in Chapter 2)
- Consultation Lineups (described in Chapter 2)
- Text posters
- Y Chart (described in Chapter 4)
- Idea Wave (described in Chapter 4)
- Flip book
- Numbered Heads Huddle (described in Chapter 4)

- Snowball (described in Chapter 4)
- Exit cards (described in Chapter 4)
- Outcome sentences (described in Chapter 4)
- Reflective writing
- Letter to the author
- Cubing (described in Chapter 5)
- I-search (an inquiry-based research process) paper extending theme
- Rewrite ending
- Debate/panel discussion
- Newspaper
- Small-group/whole-class discussion
- Story map
- Design a bulletin board to describe topic
- Construct a time line of events
- Write a "20 questions" game to play with classmates about facts and issues
- Play "Two Facts and a Fib" about content
- Illustrate a bookmark
- Make a comic strip of main events
- Write a character diary
- Do a question fan
- Write and act out a play
- Add another chapter
- Complete "Celebrate a Book" tic-tac-toe game
- Fishbone strategy

FLIP BOOK

Overview

After the students complete the reading, they are asked to reflect and connect to their learning. The Flip Book is a fun, hands-on strategy for them to summarize main events. This is a technique that provides an alternative to a traditional written book report, especially useful for the visual learners. See Figure 6.1 for Flip Book examples. Flip Books are easily made and require very little preparation.

Implementation

1. Provide the students with an 8 ½" × 11" sheet of blank paper.

2. Ask them to fold it in half lengthwise.

3. Then they fold it into fourths.

4. With a pair of scissors, they cut on the fold to the midpoint crease, creating four flaps.

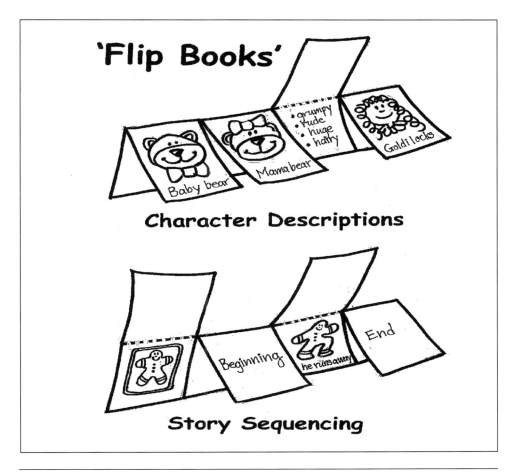

Figure 6.1   Flip Books

Source: Figure by Robert H. Perez, illustrator.

There are many ways to use a flip book as a summarizer strategy:
- Character description: Students can draw the main characters of the story on the outside flaps. Underneath the flap they list the attributes of that character.
- Story sequencing: On the outside of the flaps students write the title and the words *beginning, middle,* and *end.* Underneath the flaps students list the main events that happened at the beginning, middle, and end of the story.
- Story elements: Students write the words *character, setting, plot,* and *solution* on the outside flaps. Underneath they can use words or pictures to depict the essence of these story elements.

"TWO FACTS AND A FIB"

Overview

This is a summarizer strategy to use after the students complete the reading or lesson.

It is a summative assessment technique—similar to a true-false test with a different twist. This structure involves finding ways to honor the differences in your learners. It allows your students to show you and others what they know in many different ways.

In teams, each student writes three statements: two true, one false. Students take turns sharing their statements. Teammates try to identify the fictitious statement.

Implementation

In this structure, students try to pick out the fictitious statement from a list of three statements.

1. Teammates write three statements: two true and one false.

2. One student at a time stands and reads his or her three statements to the team.

3. Working independently, each student writes down his or her best guess as to which statement is false.

4. Teammates then discuss and reach consensus on their "best guess."

5. They have cards marked "fact" and "fib" that they hold up as each statement is read.

6. The team or partner announces their choice of the false statement.

7. The standing student announces the false statement to the group or learning partner.

8. The next teammate stands to share his or her statements. The process is repeated.

This strategy provides the students with experience in narrowing choices—great for developing test-taking skills.

This strategy also provides a great review of information learned.

Variations

- To introduce this activity, try modeling it with personal statements about yourself—two true and one false. Let the students guess the fib about you.
- As a get-acquainted activity at the beginning of the year, you can have your students use this strategy, stating two unbelievable facts about themselves and one rather believable fib. It is a fun way to get to know one another and find out little-known facts about the class members.
- This activity is an excellent way to review facts in the content area subjects as well. The student posing the ideas needs to be able to locate the answer in the text if there are any challenges from his or her teammates.

- Students can write down their three statements and roam around the room sharing their list of statements with others. The student asks his or her classmates to select the false statement. If the student fools another student, the one who was fooled should sign the paper of the student who fooled him. Find out who was able to fool the most students by comparing lists.

QUESTION FAN

Overview

The Question Fan is an interactive activity for students to reflect on the story they have just read. The prompts are open-ended and can be used with any story. They utilize verbs from Bloom's Taxonomy and so are designed to build higher-level thinking skills instead of just rote answers or "yes" or "no" responses. You can differentiate student responses by color coding the levels of questions and providing different groups with different questions.

Implementation

1. Duplicate the questions for each level of Bloom's Taxonomy on a different color of cardstock. Punch a hole at the end and connect with a paper brad. This makes it easy to "fan" them out and view them at a glance.

2. After reading a common passage or the same story, you can differentiate by assigning a team to a specific colored cluster of questions. This can be based on readiness levels or used in mixed-ability groups.

3. The questions can be directed by the teacher to the whole group, or students can use these fans and take turns asking questions with a learning partner. Students could also use these fans in a reciprocal teaching situation. Another use for the Question Fan would be for literature circles or book clubs in the classroom. Students can utilize these fans to question one another. Fans can also be made for parents to interact with their child during story time at home.

Following are examples of question prompts that correspond to Bloom's Taxonomy:

KNOWLEDGE

When and where does this story take place?

What is the problem in the story?

How does the story end?

COMPREHENSION

Explain why the story has the title it does.

How did the main character feel at the beginning of the story? At the end?

How was the problem in the story solved?

APPLICATION

If you had to cook a meal for the main character, what would you cook?

What would your mother do if she were in the story?

What would you do if you could go where the story takes place?

ANALYSIS

What do you do that is just like what the person in the story did?

What things in the story could really happen?

What part of the story was funniest? Or the saddest? Or the most exciting?

EVALUATION

Compare two of the characters.

Would you recommend this book to a friend? Why or why not?

Was the main character in the story good or bad? Explain your answer.

SYNTHESIS

Think of two to three new titles that give a good idea of what the story was about.

Retell the story from another character's (such as an animal's) point of view.

How else could the story have ended?

CELEBRATE A BOOK

Overview

Celebrate a Book is an open-ended activity for students to reflect on the story they have just read. The prompts celebrate the unique learning styles of all of your students. Students are given choices of products to show what they know after reading a book.

Implementation

1. Design a tic-tac-toe grid like Figure 6.2 on page 108 with tasks to be accomplished, outcomes, or products to do after reading a story or a book. For example:

- Write a newspaper article about the events in the book.
- Write a letter to the author telling what you thought of the book.
- Give a persuasive speech to convince someone to read the book.
- Create a story map for the book.

2. Student chooses three ways to celebrate a book that will give them tic-tac-toe.

3. Make sure that the students can only get tic-tac-toe by going through the center square—that is, they need to make a story map.

FISHBONE STRATEGY

Overview

This is a comprehension strategy that reinforces important information by asking the *who, what, when, where, why,* and *how* questions in addition to stating the *main idea.* It is an interactive note-taking structure that is valuable in research or for summarizing important information. The unique recording format supports students' writing by providing an organizational framework.

The Fishbone technique is a form of graphic organizer that allows students to report and record essential elements of a narrative or informational text. It is particularly helpful when the reading material is sequential.

With the Fishbone shape as the organizer, students are asked to identify *who, what, when, where, why, how,* and the main idea. See Figure 6.3 on page 109 for a Fishbone organizer. Benefits of using this organizer include:

Helping students remember important information within a chapter or story by asking comprehension questions.

Providing a structure for note taking for future study.

Supporting a student's writing by providing a format that lends itself to sentence writing.

Implementation

1. The teacher should model this strategy after reading a short passage to the class. The modeling process is critical to student success. The students need to see how the information is recorded.

2. Using an overhead transparency of the Fishbone pattern, the teacher displays the basic questions (*who, what, when, where, how and why*) that need to be answered about the selected text.

3. Students are given the reading assignment and instructed to look for the six basic questions as they read the text. Encourage the students to take notes as they read.

Celebrate a Book Tic-Tac-Toe

Choose three ways to celebrate a book that will give you tic-tac-toe. You can only get tic-tac-toe by going through the center box.

Produce a puppet show retelling the story.	Pretend you are a reporter covering an event from the story and write a newspaper article.	Memorize a passage from the story; present to class with background music.
Pretend you are a set designer and draw/construct several settings from your story.	Complete a story map.	Write a letter to the author telling how you felt about the book.
Give a persuasive speech to "sell" the book.	Role-play some parts of the story that have heavy dialogue.	Pantomime a part of the story so other groups can guess story part.

Figure 6.2 Celebrate a Book

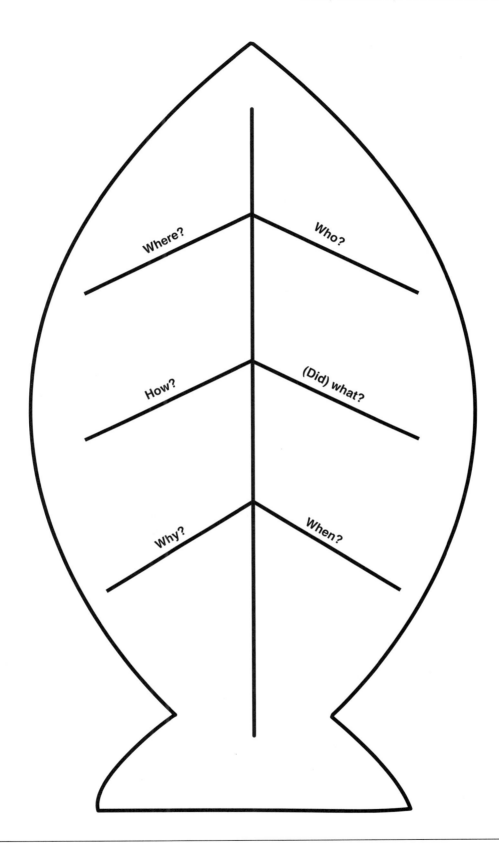

Figure 6.3   Fishbone Strategy

4. As the students read, they are encouraged to fill in the answers to the six basic questions. Let them know that the author doesn't always supply all the necessary information, so the Fishbone may have some "gaps." Sometimes the information can be inferred from other information provided.

5. After the students have completed the reading and the Fishbone pattern, they are asked to write the main idea of the passage. You can ask your students: "What one statement can you make that describes what the author is telling us?"

Variations

Questions Reflecting Literary Elements

Who?	The characters
What?	The acts or actions occurring
When?	The time
Where?	The physical setting or location
Why?	The motive or reason
How?	The method/quality associated with the action (Example: *anxiously* *waited*)
Main Idea	The major theme or conflict presented

Questions in Expanded Format

Who?	Who was involved?
What?	What did this person or group do?
When?	When was it done?
Where?	Where was it done?
Why?	Why did it happen?
How?	How was it accomplished?

Adaptations

The Fishbone strategy is designed as an independent or collaborative activity for upper grades or secondary students. The teacher, as part of an oral discussion, could easily model it for primary students where information from a story is recorded. Primary students could also use pictures when recording their answers. Another variation would be to show pictures after reading a selection and have the children decide which picture best answers one of the six questions.

QUESTION "CONNECTIONS"

Overview

Use these simple questioning stems to activate the students before, during, and after the reading.

Prereading Questions

Preview the passage. What do you think it will be about?

What are some things that you already know about this topic?

What are your reading goals?

What do you hope to learn from reading this passage?

What is your purpose for reading?

What strategies could you use as you read the passage to help you understand what you are reading?

How will you know that you understand the message intended by the author?

Questions to Ask While Reading

What do you think are the main ideas so far?

What kind of a graphic organizer would you use to begin organizing these ideas?

What did you picture in your mind about these ideas as you were reading?

Is the information in this passage similar to anything you have learned before? How?

What are you wondering about at this point in your reading? Write down your questions.

What is your attitude toward reading this passage?

Questions to Ask After Reading

What were the main ideas in this passage?

Were your predictions accurate?

What other information do you want to remember from this passage?

How will you help yourself remember this information?

Did you accomplish your reading goal?

Which reading and learning strategies did you find most helpful and why?

What parts of the passage interested you the most?

What ideas made you think?

How has your thinking changed as a result of reading this passage?

What kind of a graphic organizer would you use to depict what you remember?

CONCLUSION

Using Strategies Effectively

Teachers are always on the lookout for new materials, resources, and practical ideas to use in their classrooms. It is one thing to hear or see a strategy demonstrated in a workshop by a consultant, and it is another thing to translate it into use in your classroom. It is my hope that this book provides you with easy-to-use strategies that can be utilized across the curriculum. Keep in mind that what the student is learning is more important than which strategy is used. Make sure that the teaching strategy is aligned with your learning goals. With reading comprehension, it is the students' thinking that counts. Just following the guidelines of a strategy does not guarantee that the students will engage in higher-level thinking. Be on alert for students who are just "doing" instead of engaging in thinking about what they read. Adjust what you are doing to match your students' and your goals. Be flexible and adjust the strategies to fit your needs.

References

Allington, R. L. (2002). *Schools that work: Where all children read and write.* Boston: Allyn & Bacon.

Armstrong, T. (2000). *Multiple intelligences in the classroom* (2nd ed.). Alexandria, VA: ASCD.

Armstrong, T. (2003). *Multiple intelligences of reading and writing: Making the words come alive.* Alexandria, VA: ASCD.

Bergen, D., & Coscia, J. (2001). *Brain research and childhood education: Implications for educators.* Olney, MD: Association for Childhood Education International.

Blachowicz, C., & Fisher, P. J. (2002). *Teaching vocabulary in all classrooms* (2nd ed.). Upper Saddle River, NJ: Merrill Prentice Hall.

Brandt, R. (1997). On using knowledge about our brain: A conversation with Bob Sylwester. *Educational Leadership, 54,* 16–19.

Brandt, R. (1998). *Powerful learning.* Alexandria, VA: ASCD.

Buehl, D. (2001). *Classroom strategies for interactive learning* (2nd ed.). Newark, DE: IRA.

Burmark, L. (2002). *Visual literacy: Learn to see, see to learn.* Alexandria, VA: ASCD.

Caine, R., & Caine, G. (1997). *Education on the edge of possibility.* Alexandria, VA: ASCD.

Caine, R., & Caine, G. (1997). *Unleashing the power of perceptual change: The potential of brain-based teaching.* Alexandria, VA: ASCD.

Caine, R. N. (2000). Building the bridge from research to classroom. *Educational Leadership, 58,* 59–61.

Campbell, L. (1997). Variations on a theme: How teachers interpret MI theory. *Educational Leadership, 55,* 14–19.

Caulfield, J., Kidd, S., & Kocher, T. (2000). Brain-based instruction in action. *Educational Leadership, 58,* 62–65.

Church, E. B. (2002). *50 fun & easy brain-based activities for young learners.* New York: Scholastic Professional Books.

Ciardiello, A. V. (1998). Did you ask a good question today? Alternative cognitive and meta-cognitive strategies. *Journal of Adolescent & Adult Literacy, 39,* 190–199.

Cobb, C. D., & Mayer, J. D. (2000). Emotional intelligence: What the research says. *Educational Leadership, 58,* 14–18.

Cohen, J. (Ed.). (1999). *Education minds and hearts: Social emotional learning and the passage into adolescence.* Alexandria, VA: ASCD.

Costa, A. (Ed.). (2001). *Developing minds: A resource book for teaching thinking.* Alexandria, VA: ASCD.

Costa, A. L., & Kallick, B. (2000). *Discovering & exploring habits of mind.* Alexandria, VA: ASCD.

Cotton, K. (2000). *The schooling practices that matter most.* Alexandria, VA: ASCD.

Cowan, G., & Cowan, E. (1980). *Writing.* New York: John Wiley.

D'Arcangelo, M. (2000). How does the brain develop? A conversation with Steven Peterson. *Educational Leadership, 58,* 68–71.

Delpit, L. (1995). *Other people's children: Cultural conflict in the classroom.* New York: New Press.

Devinsky, O., & D'Esposito, M. (2004). *Neurology of cognitive and behavioral disorders.* Oxford, UK: Oxford University Press.

Diamond, M., & Hopson, J. (1998). *Magic trees of the mind: How to nurture your child's intelligence, creativity, and healthy emotions from birth through adolescence.* New York: Penguin Putnam.

Douville, R., & Wood, K. D. (2001). Collaborative learning strategies in diverse classrooms. In V. J. Risko & K. Bromley (Eds.), *Collaboration for diverse learners: Viewpoints and practices* (pp. 123–151). Newark, DE: IRA.

Duffy-Hester, A. (1999). Teaching struggling readers in elementary school classrooms: A review of classroom reading programs and principles for instruction. *Reading Teacher, 52,* 480–495.

Edwards, B. (1989). *Drawing on the right side of the brain.* New York: Penguin Putnam.

Emig, V. (1997). A multiple intelligences inventory. *Educational Leadership, 55,* 47–50.

Erlauer, L. (2003). *The brain-compatible classroom: Using what we know about learning to improve teaching.* Alexandria, VA: ASCD.

Ferguson, D. L., Ralph, G., Meyer, G., Lester, J., Droege, C., Guuyonsdottir, H., et al. (2001). *Designing personalized learning for every student.* Alexandria, VA: ASCD.

Fogarty, R. (2001). *Brain compatible classrooms* (2nd ed.). Thousand Oaks, CA: Corwin Press.

Gambrell, L. B., & Almasi, J. F. (Eds.). *Lively discussions! Fostering engaged reading.* Newark, DE: IRA.

Gardner, H. (1983). *Frames of mind: The theory of multiple intelligences.* New York: Basic Books.

Gardner, H. (1999). *Intelligence reframed: Multiple intelligences for the 21st century.* New York: Basic Books.

Guild, P. (1997). Where do the learning theories overlap? *Educational Leadership, 55,* 30–31.

Guthrie, J. T., & Wigfield, A. (Eds.). (1997). *Reading engagement: Motivating readers through integrated instruction.* Newark, DE: IRA.

Hannaford, C. (1995). *Smart moves: Why learning is not all in your head.* Arlington, VA: Great Ocean.

Hargreaves, A. (Ed.). (1997). *Rethinking educational change with heart and mind.* Alexandria, VA: ASCD.

Harmin, M. (1995). *Strategies to inspire active learning: Complete handbook.* Edwardsville, IL: Inspiring Strategy Institute.

Healy, J. (1994). *Your child's growing mind: A practical guide to brain development and learning from birth to adolescence.* New York: Doubleday.

Herber, H. (1978). *Teaching reading in content areas* (2nd ed.). Englewood Cliffs, NJ: Prentice Hall.

Hotvedt, R. (2001). In the arts spotlight. *Educational Leadership, 59,* 70–73.

Hyerle, D. (1996). *Visual tools for constructing knowledge.* Alexandria, VA: ASCD.

Ivey, G. (2000). Redesigning reading instruction. *Educational Leadership, 58,* 42–45.

Jensen, E. (1997). *Brain compatible strategies.* Del Mar, CA: Turning Point.

Jensen, E. (1998). *Teaching with the brain in mind.* Alexandria, VA: ASCD.

Jensen, E. (2000). *Different brains, different learners: How to reach the hard to reach.* Thousand Oaks, CA: Corwin Press.

Jensen, E. (2001). *Arts with the brain in mind.* Alexandria, VA: ASCD.

Johnson, D. W., & Johnson, R. T. (1999). *Learning together and alone: Cooperative, competitive, and individualistic learning.* Boston: Allyn & Bacon.

Klemp, R. (1994). Word storm: Connecting vocabulary to the student's database. *The Reading Teacher, 48,* 282.

Langer, E. (1997). *The power of mindful learning.* Reading, MA: Addison-Wesley.

LeDoux, J. (1996). *The emotional brain: The mysterious underpinnings of emotional life.* New York: Simon & Schuster.

Leff, H., & Nevin, A. (1994). *Turning learning inside out: A guide for using any subject to enrich life and creativity.* Tucson, AZ: Zephyr Press.

Levine, M. (2002). *A mind at a time.* New York: Simon & Schuster.

Lyons, C. A. (2003). *Teaching struggling readers: How to use brain-based research to maximize learning.* Portsmouth, NH: Heinemann.

Marzano, R. J. (2003). *What works in school: Translating research into action.* Alexandria, VA: ASCD.

Marzano, R. J., Pickering, D. J., & Pollock, J. E. (2001). *Classroom instruction that works: Research-based strategies for increasing student achievement.* Alexandria, VA: ASCD.

McGeehan, J. R. (Ed.). (1999). *Transformations: Leadership for brain-compatible learning.* Kent, WA: Books for Educators.

McGinley, W., & Denner, P. (1987). Story impressions: A pre-reading/writing activity. *Journal of Reading, 31,* 248–253.

Meyer, A., & Rose, D. H. (2000). Universal design for individual differences. *Educational Leadership, 58,* 39–43.

National Reading Panel. (2000). *Report of the National Reading Panel: Teaching children to read: An evidence based assessment of the scientific research literature on reading and its implications for reading instruction.* Washington, DC: National Institute of Child Health and Development.

Ogle, D. (1986). K-W-L: A teaching model that develops active reading of expository text. *Reading Teacher, 39,* 564–570.

Ogle, D. M. (1992). KWL in action: Secondary teachers find applications that work. In E. K. Dishner, T. W. Bean, J. E. Readence, & D. W. Moore (Eds.), *Reading in the content areas: Improving classroom instruction* (3rd ed., pp. 270–281). Dubuque, IA: Kendall-Hunt.

Opitz, M. F. (1998). *Literacy instruction for culturally and linguistically diverse students.* Newark, DE: IRA.

Poole, C. (1997). Maximizing learning: A conversation with Renate Nummela Caine. *Educational Leadership, 54,* 11–15.

Restak, R. (1979, 1988). *The brain.* New York: Warner Books.

Ronis, D. (2000). *Brain-compatible assessments.* Thousand Oaks, CA: Corwin Press.

Saphier, J., & Haley, M. A. (1993). *Activators: Activity structures to engage students' thinking before instruction.* Carlisle, MA: Research for Better Teaching.

Shaywitz, S. (2003). *Overcoming dyslexia.* New York: Random House.

Shore, R. (1997). *Rethinking the brain: New insights into early development.* New York: Families and Work Institute.

Silver, H., Strong, R., & Perini, M. (1997). Integrating learning styles and multiple intelligences. *Educational Leadership, 55,* 22–27.

Silver, H., Strong, R., & Perini, M. (2000). *So each may learn: Integrating learning styles and multiple intelligences.* Alexandria, VA: ASCD.

Smilkstein, R. (2003). *We're born to learn: Using the brain's natural learning process to create today's curriculum.* Thousand Oaks, CA: Corwin Press.

Sousa, D. (1998). *Learning manual for how the brain learns.* Thousand Oaks, CA: Corwin Press.

Sousa, D. (2005). *How the brain learns to read.* Thousand Oaks, CA: Corwin Press.

Sprenger, M. (1999). *Learning & memory: The brain in action.* Alexandria, VA: ASCD.

Sprenger, M. (2002). *Becoming a "wiz" at brain-based teaching: How to make every year your best year.* Thousand Oaks, CA: Corwin Press.

Stone, J., & Kagan, S. (1994). *Cooperative learning & language arts.* San Juan Capistrano, CA: Kagan Cooperative Learning.

Sylwester, R. (1995). *A celebration of neurons: An educator's guide to the human brain.* Alexandria, VA: ASCD.

Sylwester, R. (2000). Unconscious emotions, conscious feelings. *Educational Leadership, 58,* 20–24.

Tomlinson, C. (2001). *How to differentiate instruction in mixed-ability classrooms.* Alexandria, VA: ASCD.

Umstatter, J. (1996). *Brain games! Ready-to-use activities that make thinking* fun *for grades 6–12.* San Francisco, CA: John Wiley & Sons.

Vaughn, J., & Estes, T. (1986). *Reading and reasoning beyond the primary grades.* Boston: Allyn & Bacon.

Vialle, E. (1997). Multiple intelligences in multiple settings. *Educational Leadership, 55,* 65–69.

Wagmeister, J., & Shifrin, B. (2000). Thinking differently, learning differently. *Educational Leadership, 58,* 45–48.

Walsh, P. (2000). A hands-on approach to understanding the brain. *Educational Leadership, 58,* 76–78.

Westwater, A., & Wolfe, P. (2000). The brain-compatible curriculum. *Educational Leadership, 58,* 49–52.

Wolfe, P. (2001). *Brain matters: Translating research into classroom practice.* Alexandria, VA: ASCD.

Wolfe, P., & Nevilles, P. (2004). *Building the reading brain, pre k–3,* Thousand Oaks, CA: Corwin Press.

Wooten, D. A. (2000). *Valued voices: An interdisciplinary approach to teaching and learning.* Newark, DE: IRA.

VIDEOS

The brain and learning. (1998). Alexandria, VA: ASCD. #498062H01.
The brain and reading. (1999). Alexandria, VA: ASCD. #499207H01.

Index

CORWIN
PRESS

The Corwin Press logo—a raven striding across an open book—represents the union of courage and learning. Corwin Press is committed to improving education for all learners by publishing books and other professional development resources for those serving the field of PreK–12 education. By providing practical, hands-on materials, Corwin Press continues to carry out the promise of its motto: **"Helping Educators Do Their Work Better."**